CH

Contemporary Discourse
in the Field of
PHYSICS™

Quantum Physics

An Anthology of Current Thought

Edited by Fannie Huang

The Rosen Publishing Group, Inc., New York

To all my past and present science professors

Published in 2006 by The Rosen Publishing Group, Inc.
29 East 21st Street, New York, NY 10010

First Edition

Library of Congress Cataloging-in-Publication Data

Quantum physics: an anthology of current thought/ edited by Fannie Huang.—1st ed.
    p. cm.—(Contemporary discourse in the field of physics)
Includes bibliographical references and index.
ISBN 1-4042-0406-7 (lib. bdg.)
1. Quantum theory—History. 2. Physics—History.
I. Huang, Fannie. II. Series.
QC173.98.Q36 2006
530.12—dc22

                                            2004026413

Manufactured in the United States of America

On the cover: On the front cover (clockwise from top right): Patterns of light on a white surface; quantum bubbles; portrait of Sir Isaac Newton; liquid crystal.

CONTENTS

Introduction

The digital age has revolutionized the way we think, communicate, work, and enjoy life. Technology has increased the pace of life at an astounding rate, giving us greater capabilities to accomplish more in a single day than ever before imaginable. Increased access to knowledge continues to fuel the scientific drive for discovery, and the future of technology now seems limitless. The transformation of our lifestyles by technology would not have advanced as it did without the revolutionary paradigm of quantum theory. This theory enables scientists to break down nature into explicit detail, and hence equips us with the knowledge to manipulate and build designer devices that have only begun to transform our existence.

Quantum theory is based on the idea that energy exists in discrete quantifiable states. The classic example of discrete energy states is that of a burning flame, in which distinct colors represent each energy level. Max Planck (1858–1947) made this initial discovery in 1900, and introduced quantum ideas to the field of physics. Although the theory challenged the classical view of physics that energy flows continuously, Planck's novel ideas intrigued enough physicists to lead twentieth-century science into a whole new realm. Quantum theory explained the particle behavior of photons as well as the orbital nature of atomic structure by describing quantized energy states. With these founding discoveries, quantum physics embarked on a fascinating tour of the natural world.

The evolving nature of science is driven by the desire to bring theory closer to truth. In the early 1900s, as physicists tested quantum ideas and theories with experiments and mathematical proofs, they laid the founding principles for describing particle behavior and established the rules of quantum mechanics. These rules assign values to properties such as the position, momentum, and energy of a particle. Quantum physics was used to explain the existence of matter and how particles interact with each other on a microscopic scale. Physicists could now explain the organization of the periodic table of elements in terms of energy states for electrons. They could also predict the position of an electron in terms of its spin, albeit with a certain degree of uncertainty. In 1927, the essence of quantum physics was born with the Heisenberg uncertainty principle, which states that in any measurement of a property of a particle, there exists an uncertainty that cannot be overcome by an experimental observer. Thus, what happens in reality in the absence of an observer can never be definitively known. The establishment of these founding principles has been called the first quantum revolution. As physicists began to apply these rules to various systems and gain knowledge about molecular interactions on a universal level, the immense power of quantum physics was realized.

Scientific revolutions are often followed by a period of rapid productivity, when mysteries are unraveled based on the founding principles of a revolutionary new theory. This was certainly true concerning quantum theory. It didn't take long for scientists to expand quantum theory into many different directions, producing several subtheories on cosmology, black holes, space, and time to help us better understand how nature works. The subtheories have gone through numerous revisions, debates, and transformations—from string theory to superstring theory to the all-encompassing M-theory.

Meanwhile, the search continues for the ideal theory to explain natural phenomena, such as gravity, using quantum ideas. Future work in quantum physics is aimed at using quantum physics for the teleportation of objects and the understanding of time travel, two concepts that once only seemed possible in science-fiction fantasies. Quantum physics makes these feats possible in theory, and now experiments are under way to bring theory closer to reality.

As the first quantum revolution continued making valuable contributions to the pool of scientific knowledge, the buildup for a second quantum revolution was already under way. This time the revolution would be a technological one, one that we are still in the midst of experiencing. For example, quantum physics has helped explain the phenomenon of superconductivity—the ability of certain materials to conduct electric fields without the loss of any energy through resistance. Superconductivity has been translated into technological advances through the development of devices such as ultrafast computer chips and magnetic resonance imaging (MRI) machines.

Quantum physicists have continued to break down atomic particles into even smaller components, such as hadrons and quarks, enabling the study of particle behavior with remarkable precision. Once research scientists began to understand and explain the building blocks of matter, applied scientists and engineers were able to design atoms for specific purposes. This gave birth to the new field of nanotechnology. Devices such as computer chips can be built on a minuscule scale, with even greater capacities for information storage. Engineers also have the capability of building computers that process information using optics rather than electricity, offering an exponential increase in the speed of transmission. The application of quantum theory to the processing and storing of information is only beginning to revolutionize life around the world. Imagination and ingenuity, coupled with the growing knowledge base gained from quantum physics research, will continue to bring forward new technological wonders with endless possibilities.

Quantum physics has endured a long reputation as an abstract and intimidating field not only to readers outside the scientific community but to many physicists as well. This anthology of quantum physics concepts and applications only touches the surface of quantum theory's potential. These selections introduce the basic ideas underlying the field of quantum physics, then go on to discuss the evolution of quantum physics from theory to application.

An important feature of quantum physics is that it has been invaluable to the progress of other fields of science such as chemistry, astronomy, biology, and engineering. Since the inception of quantum mechanics, significant progress toward the goal of understanding the existence of matter has been made. However, as with all scientific endeavors, solutions to one set of questions give rise to new questions. With these new challenges come enormous possibilities. With persistence and dedication to the scientific method, quantum physics will lead us to a greater understanding of the universe and our place within it. —*FH*

1 Origins of Quantum Physics

In the early 1900s, the founding ideas of quantum theory sparked a revolutionary concept that would have a profound impact on everyday life in the twenty-first century. At an exponential rate, scientific knowledge has been translated into elements of our daily lives, most notably the electronic computer. The digital age would not exist as it does today without the persistence and brilliance of physicists who contributed to the advent of quantum physics.

In his book Visions: How Science Will Revolutionize the 21st Century, *prominent theoretical physicist Michio Kaku describes the integral part that science will play in our future. In the introductory chapter that follows, Kaku provides the reader with a sense of how science, and more specifically how quantum physics, has laid the groundwork for important discoveries at the turn of the millennium and will continue to bring forth new and exciting developments in the future.* —FH

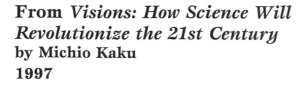

From *Visions: How Science Will Revolutionize the 21st Century*
by Michio Kaku
1997

Three centuries ago, Isaac Newton wrote: ".. . to myself I seem to have been only like a boy playing on a seashore, and diverting myself in now and then finding a smoother pebble or a prettier shell than ordinary, whilst the great ocean of truth lay all undiscovered before me." When Newton surveyed the vast ocean of truth which lay before him, the laws of nature were shrouded in an impenetrable veil of mystery, awe, and superstition. Science as we know it did not exist.

Life in Newton's time was short, cruel, and brutish. People were illiterate for the most part, never owned a book or entered a classroom, and rarely ventured beyond several miles of their birthplace. During the day, they toiled at backbreaking work in the fields under a merciless sun. At night, there was usually no entertainment or relief to comfort them except the empty sounds of the night. Most people knew firsthand the gnawing pain of hunger and chronic, debilitating disease. Most people would live not much longer than age thirty, and would see many of their ten or so children die in infancy.

But the few wondrous shells and pebbles picked up by Newton and other scientists on the seashore helped to trigger a marvelous chain of events. A profound transformation occurred in human society. With Newton's mechanics came powerful machines, and eventually the steam engine, the motive force which reshaped the world by overturning agrarian society, spawning factories and stimulating commerce, unleashing the industrial revolution, and opening up entire continents with the railroad.

By the nineteenth century, a period of intense scientific discovery was well underway. Remarkable advances in science and medicine helped to lift people out of wretched poverty and ignorance, enrich their lives, empower them with knowledge, open their eyes to new worlds, and eventually unleash complex forces which would topple the feudal dynasties, fiefdoms, and empires of Europe.

By the end of the twentieth century, science had reached the end of an era, unlocking the secrets of the atom, unraveling the molecule of life, and creating the electronic computer. With these three fundamental discoveries, triggered by the quantum revolution, the DNA revolution, and the computer revolution, the basic laws of matter, life, and computation were, in the main, finally solved.

That epic phase of science is now drawing to a close; one era is ending and another is only beginning.

This book is about this new dynamic era of science and technology which is now unfolding before our eyes. It focuses on science in the next 100 years, and beyond. The next era of science promises to be an even deeper, more thoroughgoing, more penetrating one than the last.

Clearly, we are on the threshold of yet another revolution. Human knowledge is doubling every ten years. In the past decade, more scientific knowledge has been created than in all of human history. Computer power is doubling every eighteen months. The Internet is doubling every year. The number of DNA sequences we can analyze is doubling every two years. Almost daily, the headlines herald new advances in computers, telecommunications, biotechnology, and space exploration. In the wake of this technological upheaval, entire industries and lifestyles are being overturned, only to give rise to entirely new ones. But these rapid, bewildering changes are not just quantitative. They mark the birth pangs of a new era.

Today, we are again like children walking on the seashore. But the ocean that Newton knew as a boy has largely disappeared. Before us lies a new ocean, the ocean of endless scientific possibilities and applications, giving us the potential for the first time to manipulate and mold these forces of Nature to our wishes.

For most of human history, we could only watch, like bystanders, the beautiful dance of Nature. But today, we are on the cusp of an epoch-making transition, from *being passive observers of Nature to being active choreographers of Nature*. It is this tenet that forms the central message of *Visions*. The era now unfolding makes this one of the most exciting times to be alive, allowing us to reap the fruits of the last 2,000 years of science. The Age of Discovery in science is coming to a close, opening up an Age of Mastery.

Emerging Consensus Among Scientists

What will the future look like? Science fiction writers have sometimes made preposterous predictions about the decades ahead, from vacationing on Mars to banishing all diseases. And even in the popular press, all too often an eccentric social critic's individual prejudices are substituted for the consensus within the scientific community. (In 1996, for example, *The New York Times Magazine* devoted an entire issue to life in the next 100 years. Journalists, sociologists, writers, fashion designers, artists, and philosophers all submitted their thoughts. Remarkably, *not a single scientist* was consulted.)

The point here is that predictions about the future made by professional scientists tend to be based much more substantially on the realities of scientific knowledge than those made by social critics, or even those by scientists of the past whose predictions were made before the fundamental scientific laws were completely known.

It is, I think, an important distinction between *Visions*, which concerns an emerging consensus among the scientists themselves, and the predictions in the popular press made almost exclusively by writers, journalists, sociologists, science fiction writers, and others who are *consumers* of technology, rather than by those who have helped to shape and *create* it. (One is reminded of the prediction made by Admiral William Leahy to President Truman in 1945: "That is the biggest fool thing we have ever done. . . The [atomic] bomb will never go off, and I will speak as an expert in explosives." The admiral, like many "futurists" today, was substituting his own prejudices for the consensus of physicists working on the bomb.)

As a research physicist, I believe that physicists have been particularly successful at predicting the broad outlines of the future. Professionally, I work in one of the most fundamental areas of physics, the quest to complete Einstein's dream of a "theory of everything." As a result, I am constantly reminded of the ways in which quantum physics touches many of the key discoveries that shaped the twentieth century.

In the past, the track record of physicists has been formidable: we have been intimately involved with introducing a host of pivotal inventions (TV, radio, radar, X-rays, the transistor, the computer, the laser, the atomic bomb), decoding the DNA molecule, opening new dimensions in probing the body with PET, MRI, and CAT scans, and even designing the Internet and the World Wide Web. Physicists are by no means seers who can foretell the future (and we certainly haven't been spared our share of silly predictions!). Nonetheless, it is true that some of the shrewd observations and penetrating insights of leading physicists in the history of science have opened up entirely new fields.

There undoubtedly will be some astonishing surprises, twists of fate, and embarrassing gaps in this vision of the future: I will almost inevitably overlook some important inventions and discoveries of the twenty-first century. But by focusing on the interrelations between the three great scientific revolutions, and by consulting with the scientists who are actively bringing about this revolution and examining their discoveries, it is my hope that we can see the direction of science in the future with considerable insight and accuracy.

Over the past ten years, while working on this book, I have had the rare privilege of interviewing over 150 scientists, including a good many Nobel Laureates, in part during the course of preparing a weekly national science radio program and producing science commentaries.

These are the scientists who are tirelessly working in the trenches, who are laying the foundations of the twenty-first century, many of whom are opening up new avenues and vistas for scientific discovery. In these interviews, as well as through my own work and research, I was able to go back over the vast panorama of science laid out before me and draw from a wide variety of expertise and knowledge. These scientists have graciously opened their offices and their laboratories and shared their most intimate scientific ideas with me. In this book, I've tried to return the favor by capturing the raw excitement and vitality of their scientific discoveries, for it is essential to instill the romance and excitement of science in the general public, especially the young, if democracy is to remain a vibrant and resonating force in an increasingly technological and bewildering world.

The fact is that there *is* a rough consensus emerging among those engaged in research about how the future will evolve. Because the laws behind the quantum theory, computers, and molecular biology are now well established, it is possible for scientists to generally predict the paths of scientific progress in the future. *This is the central reason why the predictions made here, I feel, are more accurate than those of the past.*

What is emerging is the following.

The Three Pillars of Science

Matter. Life. The Mind.

These three elements form the pillars of modern science. Historians will most likely record that the crowning achievement of twentieth-century science was unraveling the basic components underlying these three pillars, culminating in the splitting of the nucleus of the atom, the decoding of the nucleus of the cell, and the development of the electronic computer. With our basic understanding of matter and life largely complete, we are witnessing the close of one of the great chapters in the history of science. (This does not mean that all the laws of these three pillars are completely known, only the most fundamental. For example, although the laws of electronic computers are well known, only some of the basic laws of artificial intelligence and the brain are known.)

The first of these twentieth-century revolutions was the *quantum revolution*, the most fundamental of all. It was the quantum revolution that later helped to spawn the two other great scientific revolutions, the *biomolecular revolution* and the *computer revolution*.

The Quantum Revolution

Since time immemorial, people have speculated what the world was made of. The Greeks thought that the universe was made of four elements: water, air, earth, and fire. The philosopher Democritus believed that even these could be broken down into smaller units, which he called "atoms." But attempts to explain how atoms could create the vast, wondrous diversity of matter we see in Nature always faltered. Even Newton, who discovered the cosmic laws which guided the motion of planets and moons, was at a loss to explain the bewildering nature of matter.

All this changed in 1925 with the birth of the quantum theory, which has unleashed a thundering tidal wave of scientific discovery that continues to surge unabated to this day. The quantum revolution has now given us an almost complete description of matter, allowing us to describe the seemingly infinite multiplicity of matter we see arrayed around us in terms of a handful of particles, in the same way that a richly decorated tapestry is woven from a few colored strands.

The quantum theory, created by Erwin Schrödinger, Werner Heisenberg, and many others, reduced the mystery of matter to a few postulates. First, that energy is not continuous, as the ancients thought, but occurs in discrete bundles, called "quanta." (The photon, for example, is a quantum or packet of light.) Second, that subatomic particles have both particle and wavelike qualities, obeying a well-defined equation, the celebrated Schrödinger wave equation, which determines the probability that certain events occur. With this equation, we can mathematically predict the properties of a wide variety of substances before creating them in the laboratory. The culmination of the quantum theory is the Standard Model, which can predict the properties of everything from tiny subatomic quarks to giant supernovas in outer space.

In the twentieth century, the quantum theory has given us the ability to understand the matter we see around us. In the next century, the quantum revolution may open the door to the next step: the ability to manipulate and choreograph new forms of matter, almost at will.

From the book *Visions: How Science Will Revolutionize the 21st Century* © 1997 by Michio Kaku. Published by Anchor Books, a division of Random House. Used by permission of the Stuart Krichevsky Literary Agency, Inc.

In the year 1900, Max Planck introduced the idea of discrete quantization of energy with his work on thermal radiation. This radical idea proposed that energy does not flow continuously but jumps in steps that can be quantified, just as the different colors in a flame are distinguishable. This basic idea gave rise to a new way of thinking for physicists, and hence, new questions arose about the behavior of particles and matter. Planck's novel ideas were so confounding that it would take another twenty years before the foundations of quantum physics were established and could be applied to a variety of systems ranging from atomic to solar. Physicists are still debating the experimental evidence and interpretations of quantum physics. One hundred years later, the power of quantum physics, however, remains undisputed. Understanding the behavior of matter is the ultimate knowledge

for maneuvering through our surroundings. For example, harnessing the energy to launch a space shuttle requires an understanding of energy quanta. In this article, physics professors Daniel Kleppner and Roman Jackiw trace important early historical developments in quantum physics to help us better appreciate this revolutionary field of science. —FH

From "One Hundred Years of Quantum Physics"
by Daniel Kleppner and Roman Jackiw
Science, **2000**

An informed list of the most profound scientific developments of the 20th century is likely to include general relativity, quantum mechanics, big bang cosmology, the unraveling of the genetic code, evolutionary biology, and perhaps a few other topics of the reader's choice. Among these, quantum mechanics is unique because of its profoundly radical quality. Quantum mechanics forced physicists to reshape their ideas of reality, to rethink the nature of things at the deepest level, and to revise their concepts of position and speed, as well as their notions of cause and effect.

Although quantum mechanics was created to describe an abstract atomic world far removed from daily experience, its impact on our daily lives could hardly be greater. The spectacular advances in chemistry, biology, and medicine—and in essentially every other science—could not have occurred without the tools that quantum mechanics made possible. Without quantum mechanics there would be no global economy to speak of, because the electronics revolution that brought us the computer age is a child of quantum mechanics. So is the photonics revolution that brought us the Information Age. The creation of quantum physics has transformed our world, bringing with it all the benefits—and the risks—of a scientific revolution.

Unlike general relativity, which grew out of a brilliant insight into the connection between gravity and geometry, or the deciphering of DNA, which unveiled a new world of biology, quantum mechanics did not spring from a single step. Rather, it was created in one of those rare concentrations of genius that occur from time to time in history. For 20 years after their introduction, quantum ideas were so confused that there was little basis for progress; then a small group of physicists created quantum mechanics in three tumultuous years. These scientists were troubled by what they were doing and in some cases distressed by what they had done.

The unique situation of this crucial yet elusive theory is perhaps best summarized by the following observation: Quantum theory is the most precisely tested and most successful theory in the history of science. Nevertheless, not only was quantum mechanics deeply disturbing to its founders, today—75 years after the theory was essentially cast in its current form—some of the luminaries of science remain dissatisfied with its foundations and its interpretation, even as they acknowledge its stunning power.

This year marks the 100th anniversary of Max Planck's creation of the quantum concept. In his seminal paper on thermal radiation, Planck hypothesized that the total energy of a vibrating system cannot be changed continuously. Instead, the energy must jump from one value to another in discrete steps, or quanta, of energy. The idea of energy quanta was so radical that Planck let it lay fallow. Then, Einstein, in his wonder year of 1905, recognized the implications of quantization for light. Even then the concept was so bizarre that there was little basis for progress. Twenty more years and a fresh generation of physicists were required to create modern quantum theory.

To understand the revolutionary impact of quantum physics one need only look at prequantum physics. From 1890 to 1900, physics journals were filled with papers on atomic spectra and essentially every other measurable property of matter, such as viscosity, elasticity, electrical and thermal conductivity, coefficients of expansion, indices of refraction, and thermoelastic coefficients. Spurred by the energy of the Victorian work ethic and the development of ever more ingenious experimental methods, knowledge accumulated at a prodigious rate.

What is most striking to the contemporary eye, however, is that the compendious descriptions of the properties of matter were essentially empirical. Thousands of pages of spectral data listed precise values for the wavelengths of the elements, but nobody knew why spectral lines occurred, much less what information they conveyed. Thermal and electrical conductivities were interpreted by suggestive models that fitted roughly half of the facts. There were numerous empirical laws, but they were not satisfying. For instance, the Dulong-Petit law established a simple relation between specific heat and the atomic weight of a material. Much of the time it worked; sometimes it didn't. The masses of equal volumes of gas were in the ratios of integers—mostly. The Periodic Table, which provided a key organizing principle for the flourishing science of chemistry, had absolutely no theoretical basis.

Among the greatest achievements of the revolution is this: Quantum mechanics has provided a quantitative theory of matter. We now understand essentially every detail of atomic structure; the Periodic Table has a simple and natural explanation; and the vast arrays of spectral data fit into an elegant theoretical framework. Quantum theory permits the quantitative understanding of molecules, of solids and liquids, and of conductors and semiconductors. It explains bizarre phenomena such as superconductivity and superfluidity, and exotic forms of matter such as the stuff of neutron stars and Bose-Einstein condensates, in which all the atoms in a gas behave like a single superatom. Quantum mechanics provides essential tools for all of the sciences and for every advanced technology . . .

Quantum Mechanics

The clue that triggered the quantum revolution came not from studies of matter but from a problem in radiation.

The specific challenge was to understand the spectrum of light emitted by hot bodies: blackbody radiation. The phenomenon is familiar to anyone who has stared at a fire. Hot matter glows, and the hotter it becomes the brighter it glows. The spectrum of the light is broad, with a peak that shifts from red to yellow and finally to blue (although we cannot see that) as the temperature is raised.

It should have been possible to understand the shape of the spectrum by combining concepts from thermodynamics and electromagnetic theory, but all attempts failed. However, by assuming that the energies of the vibrating electrons that radiate the light are quantized, Planck obtained an expression that agreed beautifully with experiment. But as he recognized all too well, the theory was physically absurd, "an act of desperation," as he later described it.

Planck applied his quantum hypothesis to the energy of the vibrators in the walls of a radiating body. Quantum physics might have ended there if in 1905 a novice—Albert Einstein—had not reluctantly concluded that if a vibrator's energy is quantized, then the energy of the electromagnetic field that it radiates—light—must also be quantized. Einstein thus imbued light with particlelike behavior, notwithstanding that James Clerk Maxwell's theory, and over a century of definitive experiments, testified to light's wave nature. Experiments on the photoelectric effect in the following decade revealed that when light is absorbed its energy actually arrives in discrete bundles, as if carried by a particle. The dual nature of light—particlelike or wavelike depending on what one looks for—was the first example of a vexing theme that would recur throughout quantum physics . . .

Excerpted with permission from Dan Kleppner and Roman Jackiw. © Science, AAAS, 2000.

Quantum physics is based on the concept brought forth by Max Planck that energy jumps in discrete steps. After Planck's initial discovery of energy quanta in 1900, the next significant contribution to quantum physics came about five years later when Albert Einstein applied Planck's work to the behavior of light. Based on the photoelectric effect, Einstein theorized that light rays consisted of discrete particles called photons. According to Einstein, the energy of a photon is quantifiable and dependent only on the frequency of light. Therefore, every photon at a particular frequency has the same amount of energy, regardless of the intensity of light. This idea deviated from the previously established notion that light behaves as an infinitely continuous wave. As described by physicist and best-selling science writer Alan Lightman in the following excerpt, these conflicting theories gave rise to the particle-wave duality of light that remains a mystery to scientists even today. —FH

From "The Photoelectric Effect"
Great Ideas in Physics
by Alan P. Lightman
2000

Discovery of the Photoelectric Effect

It has been known since the late nineteenth century that under some conditions a metal releases electrons when light shines on it. This phenomenon is called the *photoelectric effect*. The number of electrons released per second can be measured by the electrical current produced in a wire connected to the metal. In addition, the kinetic energy of individual electrons can be measured by the force needed to stop them. In terms of energy, the energy of the incoming light beam is converted to the energy of the ejected electrons.

In 1902, the German experimental physicist Philipp Lenard (1862–1947) discovered a number of important properties of the photoelectric effect. First, Lenard found that a greater intensity of incoming light releases more electrons from the metal. This result was expected. If we think of the electrons as particles of sand lodged in a sandbar, then increasing the strength of an incoming wave should dislodge more sand. Secondly, Lenard found that the kinetic energy of individual escaping electrons *does not increase* when the intensity of the incoming light is increased. For light of a given frequency, the kinetic energy of each outgoing electron is *independent* of the intensity of the incoming light. This result was astonishing. Physicists had believed that the kinetic energy of individual electrons should increase with increasing light intensity, just as a stronger wave hitting a sandbar pounds each grain of sand with more force and dislodges it with more speed. Finally, Lenard found that the kinetic energy of individual escaping electrons *does* increase with increasing frequency of the incoming light wave. Quantitatively, he found the result

$$\tfrac{1}{2}mv^2 = h\boldsymbol{v} - K \qquad\qquad \text{(IV-3)}$$

where m and v are the mass and velocity of an escaping electron, $mv^2/2$ is the usual formula for kinetic energy, $\boldsymbol{v}$ is the frequency of the incoming light wave, h is a fixed number, and K is a number that varies from one metal to the next but does not depend on the incoming light. To be more precise, the velocity that occurs in Eq. (IV-3) is the maximum velocity in any large group of emerging electrons for a given metal and frequency of incoming light.

Einstein's Photon Theory of Light

Some of Lenard's discoveries were most puzzling. If light is a wave, as strongly suggested by interference phenomena, shouldn't a greater intensity of waves impart a greater energy to each ejected electron?

In 1905, the same year that he published his theory of relativity, Einstein proposed a new theory of light, a theory that explained Lenard's results. Einstein proposed that light is not distributed evenly over a region of space, as one would expect from a wave, but instead comes in individual "drops" of energy. Each drop of light is called a *photon*. Photons act like particles. A typical light beam

27

should be pictured as a flow of raindrops, with empty space between the drops, rather than as a continuous wave of water. Einstein proposed that in a light beam of frequency ν, the energy of each photon of light is

$$E = h\nu \qquad\qquad\qquad \text{(IV-6)}$$

In this new picture of light, an individual electron is hit not by a continuous stream of energy, but by an individual photon of light. Most electrons are not hit by any photons at all and so are unaffected by the incoming light. If a particular electron is struck by and absorbs a photon, it acquires the photon's energy, $h\nu$. Some of the energized electrons will bounce around in the metal and completely dissipate their energy, and some may escape the metal, with energy left over. The chance of an energized electron being struck by additional photons, which are relatively few and far between, is extremely small. Einstein interpreted the number K in Lenard's experimental result, Eq. (IV-3), to be the *minimum* energy needed for an electron to break free from the atoms in the metal. Thus an electron struck by a photon gains an energy $h\nu$ from the photon, uses up at least an energy K to escape the atom, and has a remaining kinetic energy of at most $h\nu - K$. The fastest-moving escaping electrons should then have a kinetic energy of $h\nu - K$, as found by Lenard and shown in Eq. (IV-3).

Einstein's photon theory of light explained all of Lenard's results. An increase in light intensity corresponds to a greater number of photons per second. Since each photon may eject an electron, a greater number of electrons will be ejected each second. However, for light of a fixed frequency, the energy of each photon remains the same, $E = h\nu$, and is *not* increased by increasing the intensity of light. So when a single electron is hit by a single photon, the energy gained by the electron will remain the same, regardless of the intensity of the light. There may be many more photons flying about, but an electron can be hit by only one of them at a time. On the other hand, increasing the *frequency* of the incoming light, whatever its intensity, will increase the energy of each photon of light, as described by Eq. (IV-6), and each ejected electron will gain more energy. Even if the intensity of the incoming light is decreased, so that the light is very dim, an increased frequency gives each photon more energy and thus gives each ejected electron more energy. Perhaps most strikingly, for sufficiently low frequencies of incoming light, no electrons are ejected regardless of the light intensity. This result is, in fact, observed. A high intensity of light means many photons per second, but the energy of each of those photons can still be very small if the frequency of light is low.

In Einstein's theory of light, light acts like a particle, not like a wave. The constant h is a fundamental constant of nature, meaning that it has the same value for all situations, in all places and at all times, just as the speed of light is believed to be the same everywhere in the universe. The constant h is called Planck's constant, named after the great German theoretical physicist Max Planck (1858–1947). (Planck, Lenard, and Einstein were all Nobel prize winners.) In 1901, Planck had proposed that an individual atom vibrating at a frequency ν

could emit energy not in a continuous range of energies but only in multiples of hv; that is, an atom vibrating at v cycles per second could emit an energy of $1hv$, or $2hv$, or $3hv$, and so on, but not anything less than hv and not any fractional multiple of hv. Planck had been forced to this odd proposal in an attempt to explain the observed radiation from hot objects like furnaces. From the observations, Planck was able to determine the required value of h for his theory, and it was the same as that later found in the photoelectric effect.

What Planck and Einstein suggested was that energy in nature comes not in a continuous, infinitely divisible stream but in indivisible packets. The indivisible packet of energy is called the *quantum*. The quantum of light is the photon. Analogously, the quantum of money in the United States is the cent. Every purchase involves a multiple of cents, but not fractions of cents.

Because the packet of energy, the quantum, is typically so small, we are not aware from ordinary experience that such a minimum amount exists, in the same way that we cannot see the individual grains of sand when looking at a beach from a distance of a few meters or more.

Einstein's photon theory applies to light containing several different frequencies as well as to light of a single frequency. Any composite beam of light can be broken up into its component frequencies—by a prism, for example—and each single-frequency component behaves like a group of photons of that frequency. Thus, a beam of white light, containing many different frequencies, contains photons of many different individual frequencies and individual energies.

Lenard's experimental results with the photoelectric effect and Einstein's interpretations of those results strongly suggested that light came in particles. Yet previous experiments, particularly those involving interference effects, had shown that light behaved like a wave. How could something behave both like a particle, coming in a localized unit, and like a wave, coming in a continuous and spread-out form? This self-contradictory duality dumbfounded many physicists of the day, including Planck and Einstein, and it still does.

Lightman, Alan P. *Great Ideas in Physics: The Conservation of Energy, the Second Law of Thermodynamics, the Theory of Relativity, and Quantum Mechanics* © McGraw-Hill Professional, 2000.

In the previous excerpt, Alan Lightman introduces readers to Einstein's pioneering theory of light that followed Max Planck's work on thermal radiation. The particle-wave duality of light exemplifies the essence of quantum physics in that there is an underlying uncertainty that exists when determining the precise behavior of matter. The behavior of light as a quantifiable particle as well as the behavior of light as a continuous wave can both be observed in experiments, and therefore the problem remains unresolved. Which behavior is occurring in reality? Fundamental to the understanding of particle physics is the classic double-slit experiment. First performed by

Thomas Young in the early 1800s, the experiment indicates that light, indeed, behaves as a wave. By performing the experiment, an observer can witness the wavelike nature of light because of interference effects. However, the particlelike behavior of light can be demonstrated through the use of photon detectors. While describing this contradictory experimental evidence, Lightman points out the intriguing idea that unobserved reality can be distinct from an observer's reality. —FH

From "The Double-Slit Experiment"
Great Ideas in Physics
by Alan P. Lightman
2000

Description of the Experiment

There is a simple but famous experiment that illustrates the wave-particle duality of nature in its most disturbing form. This experiment has several parts. In the first part, put a window shade with a thin horizontal slit in it between a light source and a screen, as shown in Fig. IV-6 (a). Darken the room, so that the only source of light comes from behind the shade (to the left of the shade, in the figure). Furthermore, make the source of light extremely weak, so that it emits only a few photons of light per second. Now, measure the pattern of light that hits the screen.

Next, cover up the first slit in the shade and cut a second slit above it, as shown in Fig. IV-6 (b). Repeat the experiment and measure the pattern of light on the screen. In each of these first two experiments, light can get to the screen only through one slit in the shades because only one slit is open at a time.

For the third experiment, uncover *both* slits in the shade. If light consists of particles, as the photoelectric effect and Compton's experiments show, then each photon of light coming from behind the shade and striking the screen must pass through *either* the top slit *or* the bottom slit. This seems obvious. A particle

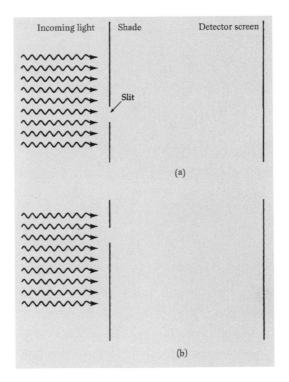

FIGURE IV-6 (a) The double-split experiment. Light is represented as waves. (b) The same as part (a), with the slit in a different location.

can't be in two places at the same time. The photons that pass through the bottom slit should produce a pattern of light on the screen that is identical to that found in the first experiment, where only the bottom slit was open. Likewise, the photons that pass through the top slit should produce a pattern of light on the screen that is identical to that found in the second experiment, where only the top slit was open. Therefore, the pattern of light on the screen in the third experiment should be the *combination* of the patterns seen in the first two experiments. Regions of the screen that were lit up in *either* of the first two experiments should be lit up in the third experiment. Regions of the screen that were dark in both of the first two experiments—that is, regions that were not struck by any photons in either experiment—should be dark in the third experiment.

These anticipated results for the third experiment will indeed be observed if we place photon detectors after the slits in the shade, as shown in Fig. IV-6 (c), to show us which slit each photon passes through. (Notice that in this figure, we have drawn the incoming light as a group of particles, rather than incoming waves.) Our detectors are designed such that they make a clicking sound each time a photon passes through them. The first such detectors able to detect individual photons were called photomultipliers and were developed in the late 1930s.

If we perform the third experiment with the two photon detectors in place, we can listen for the clicks and know for sure which slit each photon passes

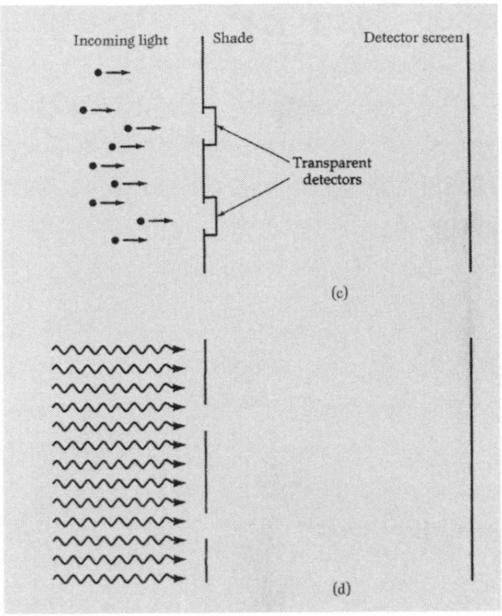

FIGURE IV-6 (c) The double-slit experiment, with both slits open and monitored by photon detectors. Here, the incoming light is represented as photons. (d) The double-slit experiment, with both slits open and without the photon detectors. Here, the incoming light is represented as waves.

through. Remember that our source of light behind the shade is extremely weak and emits only a few photons per second. With the detectors in place, we will sometimes hear one detector click, meaning a photon has just passed through it, and sometimes hear the other detector click, meaning a photon has passed through it. We never hear the two detectors click at the same time. We can literally count photons of light, one at a time, and say for certain which slit each photon passes through on its way to the screen. When we examine the screen, we will indeed find the added patterns of the first two experiments. All of this makes perfect sense and clearly suggests that light is a group of particles.

The trouble comes in the fourth experiment. Keep everything the same, but remove the two detectors, as shown in Fig. IV-6 (d). Common sense says that the pattern of light on the screen should be the same as in the previous experiment: just because we don't record which slit each photon passes through doesn't mean that the photons don't pass through the slits just as before. With or without the two detectors, the photons still must pass through the slits to illuminate the screen. However, the pattern of light on the screen *does* change. The pattern is no longer the sum of the patterns from each individual slit, found in the first two experiments. Instead, the pattern is now what we would expect from the interference of two overlapping waves emanating from the slits. (Accordingly, we have chosen to draw the incoming light in Fig. IV-6 (d) as incoming waves.) This version of the experiment was first performed about 1807 by Thomas Young, whom we have mentioned earlier.

Let's think about what this means. Interference of two waves requires that the waves overlap, that they occupy the same space. Thus, *two* waves of light must simultaneously occupy the space between the shade and the screen during the period of transit from the shade to the screen. For the sake of calculation, let's say that the shade and the screen are 1 meter apart. Since light travels with a speed of about 3×10^8

meters per second, the passage time from shade to screen is about

$$\frac{1 \text{ meter}}{3 \times 10^8 \text{ m/s}} = 3.3 \times 10^{-9} \text{ second.}$$

From this calculation, in order to produce the observed interference pattern on the screen, the two light waves, one from each slit, must be emitted no further apart in time than every 3.3×10^{-9} second, so that they will overlap on their way to the screen. However, we have made our source of light so weak that it emits only a few photons per second—let's say one photon every 0.3 second. So two successive photons cannot possibly overlap on their way from the shade to the screen. Each photon has long since emerged from the slit and traveled to the screen, in 3.3×10^{-9} second, before the next photon comes along, 0.3 second later. Furthermore, in the third experiment the two detectors never clicked at the same time, a result ruling out the possibility that the incoming photons could have divided in two and passed through both slits at the same time. In the third experiment, the time between clicks was about 0.3 second.

So we have a contradiction! The fourth experiment requires that two waves of light pass almost simultaneously through the two slits, so that they can overlap on their way to the screen and produce the observed interference pattern. The third experiment shows that two photons never pass through the two slits at the same time; each photon passes through one slit at a time, and the resulting pattern of light is in accordance with such a picture: the sum of two single-slit patterns.

The contradiction between the third and fourth experiments is the enigma of the wave-particle duality of light and, as we will show, the duality of all nature. When we don't check to see which slit each photon goes through, each photon behaves as if it went through both slits at the same time, as a spread-out wave would do. When we do check, each photon goes through *either* one slit *or* the other and behaves as a particle. Light behaves sometimes as a wave and sometimes as a particle. Astoundingly, and against all common sense, the behavior that occurs in a given experiment depends on what the experimenter chooses to measure. Evidently, the observer, and the knowledge sought by the observer, play some kind of fundamental role in the properties of the thing observed. The observer is somehow part of the system. These results call into question the long-held notion of an external reality, outside and independent of the observer. There is nothing more profound and disturbing in all of physics.

These, then, are the two enigmas of the quantum world: the wave-particle duality of nature and the strange role played by the observer. If you find these results impossible to fathom, you are in excellent company. Quantum effects continue to baffle the best physicists in the world.

Lightman, Alan P. *Great Ideas in Physics: The Conservation of Energy, the Second Law of Thermodynamics, the Theory of Relativity, and Quantum Mechanics* © McGraw-Hill Professional, 2000.

In 1913, atomic physicist Niels Bohr advanced quantum theory by describing discrete energy levels in the context of electrons in an atom. He proposed that electrons orbit around the nucleus in stationary states rather than continuously vibrating states and that they jump from one state to another. During their transitions between states, the electrons change their energy levels by emitting light. Although his ideas would later prove to be correct, they still contradicted the general consensus of thought at the time, which insisted that electrons spiral continuously toward the nucleus.

Ten years later, in his Ph.D. thesis, physicist Louis de Broglie garnered more support for Bohr's quantum atomic theory by revealing the relationship between the momentum of an electron and wavelength. Finally in 1926, Erwin Schrödinger, another pioneering quantum physicist, further developed the wave theory when he solved the equations that describe the behavior of a system through a wave function. The wave function allows the calculation of every possible configuration of an electron and the determination of probable electron states. The following excerpt from a classic book by physicist David Bohm summarizes the contributions of these great physicists to quantum theory. —FH

From *Causality and Chance in Modern Physics*
by David Bohm
1999

Origin of the Quantum Theory

. . . Another important contradiction between classical theory and experiment arose in a detailed study of the frequencies of the radiation emitted by atoms. According to classical theory, there should exist a continuous range of possible sizes of orbits of the electrons. And since each different size of orbit led in general to a different frequency of revolution of the electron around the nucleus, there should be possible a corresponding continuous range of frequencies of the light emitted. Indeed, because of the chaotic character of motion at the atomic level, a given sample of matter, such as a tube of hydrogen gas, should contain atoms with a chaotically distributed range of sizes of orbits which, because there are so many atoms (10^{20} or more), would appear practically continuous. Thus, a continuous range of frequencies of light should be emitted. In reality, however, only certain discrete frequencies are obtained experimentally.

Bohr analysed this problem very carefully, and finally was able to resolve the above contradictions with experiment (as well as a number of others which we have not mentioned here) by means of a totally new kind of hypothesis. He postulated that the continuous range of orbits permitted by classical theory were not in reality possible, and that the electron could follow only certain discrete (i.e. quantized) orbits. By postulating that among these there existed a smallest possible orbit with a lowest possible energy, he immediately explained the stability of atoms. For once the electron entered this orbit, it would not be able to lose any more energy, because no more orbits of lower energy would be available for it to go to. Thus, it would remain in this orbit until it was disturbed from outside.

If, for one reason or another, the electron were in an orbit, for example, C, with an energy E_C, higher than that in the bottom orbit, then Bohr postulated that it could jump from that orbit to a lower one, for example, B, radiating the *full* energy difference $E_C - E_B$, in one single quantum of light, with a frequency given by the Einstein relation $E_C - E_B = h\nu$. This postulate clearly has as a consequence that only discrete frequencies of light can be emitted, corresponding to the discrete jumps between the various possible energy levels.

Having resolved the contradictions between theory and experiment in a *qualitative* way, Bohr proceeded to derive a *quantitative* rule, permitting him to calculate the allowed energy levels and the corresponding frequencies of light emitted at first for hydrogen atoms, and later for a few other simple kinds of atoms. This quantitative rule permitted for these cases a prediction of the frequencies emitted with a very high order of precision. These predictions enormously increased the plausibility of the theory; for they involved such a large number of frequencies and reached such a high level of precision that it would have been difficult to believe that the agreement was a coincidence.

Thus Bohr had presented very convincing evidence in favour of the idea that not only does the energy of light come in discrete packets or quanta, but also that of electrons. Further investigations, which we shall not discuss here, established a similar discontinuity in *all* forms of energy. In other words, a basic "atomicity" of energy in general had been disclosed. The size of the basic units was, however, not the same under all possible conditions. For example, with light it was proportional to the frequency, but in atoms it depended on more complex rules.

It must be emphasized, however, that it had not been explained *why* the energy is atomic in character. The atomicity had just been *postulated*; and on the basis of this postulate, many properties of atoms and of radiation were explained, which had been in contradiction with the conclusion drawn from classical physics that the energy can vary in a continuous way. Moreover, no explanation was offered for the process by which a quantum was emitted and absorbed, during the course of which the electron obviously had to jump from one discrete orbit to another. At this level of the theory, it was merely accepted that these processes occur somehow, in a way that it was hoped would be understood better later (as it was also hoped in connection with the problem of the very existence of discrete orbits).

A first step towards a better understanding of the discrete energies of atomic orbits was made by de Broglie. De Broglie's starting-point was in the suggestion that just as light-waves had a particle-like character, atomic particles might also have a wave-like character. In doing this, he was guided by the appearance in connection with many different kinds of classical waves of sets of discrete *frequencies*. For example, a string fixed at each end must vibrate in integral multiples or "harmonics" of a certain "fundamental" frequency, determined by the length, density, and tension of the cord. Likewise, sound waves in a box can have only discrete frequencies, but these are in a more complicated relation than just that of integral multiples. In general, whenever a wave is confined to oscillate within a definite space, it may be shown to have discrete possible frequencies of oscillation.

De Broglie then postulated that there exists a new kind of wave connected with an electron. As to the precise nature of this wave, most of its properties will not be important at this level of the theory. What is important here is that if it is confined within an atom, it will have discrete frequencies of oscillation. If we now postulate that the Einstein relation, $E = h\nu$, connecting the energy of the wave to its frequency applies to these waves just as it applies to light-waves, then the *discrete frequencies* will imply *discrete energies.*

The next step was to put this qualitative theory into a more quantitative form. De Broglie did this by showing, on the basis of arguments coming from the theory of relativity, that the Einstein relation, $E = h\nu$, led to another relation, $p = h\lambda$, connecting the wave-length, λ, of these waves with the momentum, p, of the electron. When the wave-length, λ, was evaluated for an electron of a typical momentum encountered under usual experimental conditions, it was found to be of the order of atomic dimensions. Now, from experience with light and other types of waves, we already know that a wave-like character is manifested clearly only when the wave meets obstacles that are not too much larger than a wave-length in size; otherwise it goes in a practically straight line as if it were a particle. Thus at the large-scale level, de Broglie's waves would not show themselves clearly, and the electron would act as if it were nothing but a classical particle. At the atomic level, however, the wave connected with the electron would produce important new effects. Among these would be the appearance of discrete frequencies of vibration resulting from confinement of the waves within an atom. Using the relation which he had discovered ($p = h/\lambda$) and the Einstein relation, $E = h\nu$, de Broglie was then able to calculate both the frequencies and the corresponding energies of the discrete possible modes of vibration of these waves; and out of these calculations he obtained exactly the same energies as those coming from Bohr's theory. Thus, the Bohr energy levels were explicable in terms of an assumed wave, *provided that one also assumed that the energy of this wave was related to its frequency by the Einstein relation, $E = h\nu$.*

Later experiments done by Davisson and Germer on the scattering of electrons from metallic crystals disclosed a statistical pattern of strong and weak scattering very similar to the fringes obtained by passing a beam of light quanta through a set of slits. The idea was then suggested that perhaps here the waves postulated by de Broglie were manifesting themselves, and that the regular array of atoms in the crystal was playing the rôle which the set of slits plays in optical interference experiments. When the length of the assumed wave was calculated on the basis of the observed pattern of strong and weak scattering, it was found to agree with that obtained from de Broglie's theory. Thus, the conjecture that electrons have some wave-like properties received a brilliant experimental confirmation. Later, similar experiments showed that other particles, such as protons, molecules, neutrons, etc., have similar wave-like properties, which also satisfy the de Broglie relations. Thus, by now we have the point of view that *all matter* has such wave-like properties.

Meanwhile, the wave theory of de Broglie had been developed into a much more precise form by Schrödinger, who obtained a partial differential equation for these waves, which determines their future motions in much the same way that Maxwell's equations determine the future motions of waves in the electromagnetic field. Schrödinger's equations permitted the precise calculation of energy levels in a very wide variety of atomic systems, which it was not possible to treat either by Bohr's theory or by de Broglie's theory; and such calculations led to a very impressive agreement with experiment in all cases. Moreover, the Schrödinger equation permitted a continuous treatment of how the wave moves in a transition from one allowed energy level to another, and thus led to the hope that perhaps the mystery of how a transition between allowed energy levels takes place could now be solved.

At this point new and apparently somewhat paradoxical limitations on the wave theory were discovered. For Schrödinger originally proposed that the electron should be thought of as a continuous distribution of charge. The density of this charge he assumed was related to the wave amplitude ψ, by the relation, $P = |\psi|^2$. Thus, the waves of de Broglie and Schrödinger were to be interpreted as waves of electric charge. In favour of this suggestion, if the electric charge were assumed to be related to the wave amplitude in this way, then Schrödinger's equation led automatically to the conclusion that the total amount of charge would remain constant, no matter how it flowed from place to place (i.e. it would be conserved), thus demonstrating a consistent feature of the interpretation.

Unfortunately, however, the interpretation was tenable only as long as the Schrödinger wave remained confined within an atom. In free space, a simple calculation showed that, according to Schrödinger's equation, the wave must spread out rapidly over all space without limit. On the other hand, the electron is always actually found within a comparatively small region of space, so that its charge density clearly cannot in general be equal to the value, $P = |\psi|^2$, postulated by Schrödinger.

To deal with this problem, [Max] Born proposed that the wave intensity represents not an actual charge density of the electron, but rather the *probability density* that the electron, conceived of as a small localized particle, shall be found at a certain place. Thus, the fact that the wave amplitude for a free electron spreads out over all space is no longer in contradiction with the appearance of the electron itself at a certain place. The conservation of $|\psi|^2$ can then be interpreted in terms of the fact that the total probability that the particle can be found somewhere in space must remain equal to unity with the passing of time.

It was not experimentally feasible to verify Born's hypothesis *directly* by observing the locations of particles in a statistical aggregate, but it was possible to verify it *indirectly*. Thus, in a transition between allowed energy levels, the change of the Schrödinger wave from one mode of vibration to another now had to be interpreted in terms of a continuously changing probability that the electron had one energy or the other.* Thus, it was possible to calculate *probabilities of transition* between energy levels under various conditions; and these probabilities were found to be in agreement with experiment. So much indirect evidence in favour of Born's hypothesis has by now been accumulated that physicists generally accept Born's interpretation of the Schrödinger wave function, ψ, as being correct.

Hence, the problem of describing what actually happens in an individual transition process had not yet been solved. With the interpretation of Born, the Schrödinger wave only treated the mean behaviour in a statistical ensemble of cases.

Bohm, David. *Causality and Chance in Modern Physics*, 1999 © Routledge.

2 Principles of Quantum Theory

Between 1925 and 1927, the most profound work in quantum physics propelled the new theory into vast acceptance. At the height of this revolutionary period, physicist Werner Heisenberg established the Heisenberg uncertainty relations. These relations helped define the position, momentum, and energy of a particle at a specific time. Classical physicists believed that these properties could be precisely measured, and the accuracy of the measurements depended on the quality of the equipment they used. However, the reality, according to Heisenberg, is that no matter how accurate your instruments are, the measurement of two properties at the same time will have a certain degree of uncertainty. In his book, Uncertainty: The Life and Science of Werner Heisenberg, science historian David Cassidy describes the work of Werner Heisenberg and why it became central to quantum physics. The following excerpt from the American Institute of Physics Web *site briefly describes some key points from Cassidy's book. —FH*

From "Quantum Mechanics, 1925–1927"
by David Cassidy and the Center for History of Physics
American Institute of Physics Web Site, 1998

The Uncertainty Principle

"The more precisely the position is determined, the less precisely the momentum is known in this instant, and vice versa."

—Heisenberg, uncertainty paper, 1927

This is a succinct statement of the "uncertainty relation" between the position and the momentum (mass times velocity) of a subatomic particle, such as an electron. This relation has profound implications for such fundamental notions as causality and the determination of the future behavior of an atomic particle.

Because of the scientific and philosophical implications of the seemingly harmless sounding uncertainty relations, physicists speak of an *uncertainty principle*, which is often called more descriptively the "principle of indeterminacy." This page focuses on the *origins* of Heisenberg's uncertainty relations and principle.

The Uncertainty Relations

Following Heisenberg's derivation of the uncertainty relations, one starts with an electron moving all by itself through empty space. To describe the electron, a physicist would refer to certain measured properties of the particle. Four of these measured properties are important for the uncertainty principle. They are the position of the electron, its momentum (which is the electron's mass times its velocity), its energy, and the time. These properties appear as "variables" in equations that describe the electron's motion.

The uncertainty relations have to do with the measurement of these four properties; in particular, they have to do with the precision with which these properties can be measured. Up until the advent of quantum mechanics, everyone thought that the precision of any measurement was limited only by the accuracy of the instruments the experimenter used. Heisenberg showed that no matter how accurate the instruments used, quantum mechanics limits the precision when two properties are measured at the same time. These are not just any two properties but two that are represented by variables that have a special relationship in the equations. The technical term is "canonically conjugate" variables. For the moving electron, the canonically conjugate variables are in two pairs: momentum and position are one pair, and energy and time are another. Roughly speaking, the relation between momentum and position is like the relation between energy and time.

The uncertainty relations involve the uncertainties in the measurements of these variables. The "uncertainty"—sometimes called the "imprecision"—is related to the range of the results of repeated measurements taken for a given variable. For example, suppose you measure the length of a book with a meter stick. It turns out to be 23.6 cm, or 23 centimeters and 6 millimeters. But since the meter stick measures only to a maximum precision of 1 mm, another measurement of the book might yield 23.7 cm or 23.5 cm. In fact, if you perform the measurement many times, you will get a "bell curve" of measurements centered on an average value, say 23.6 cm. The spread of the bell curve, or the "standard deviation," will be about 1 mm on each side of the average. This means that the "uncertainty" or the precision of the measurement is plus or minus 1 mm.

The uncertainty relations may be expressed in words as follows. "The simultaneous measurement of two conjugate variables (such as the momentum and position or the energy and time for a moving particle) entails a limitation on the precision (standard deviation) of each measurement. Namely: the more precise the measurement of position, the more imprecise the measurement of momentum, and vice versa. In the most extreme case, absolute precision of one variable would entail absolute imprecision regarding the other."

The uncertainty relations can be written a little more precisely in the shorthand of mathematical symbols. But first we must define what these symbols stand for. Here are their definitions:

Δq is the uncertainty or imprecision (standard deviation) of the position measurement.

Δp is the uncertainty of the momentum measurement in the q direction at the same time as the q measurement.

ΔE is the uncertainty in the energy measurement.

Δt is the uncertainty in the time measurement at the same time as the energy is measured.

h is a constant from quantum theory known as Planck's constant, a very tiny number.

π is pi from the geometry of circles.

≥ means "greater than or equal to"

Putting these symbols together, the two uncertainty relations look like this:

$$\Delta p \, \Delta q \geq h / 4\pi \text{ and } \Delta E \, \Delta t \geq h / 4\pi$$

Let's say you measure the position of a moving electron with such great accuracy that Δq is very small. What happens to the precision of the momentum Δp, which you measure at the same instant? From the first relation, we have

$$\Delta p \geq h / 4\pi \Delta q$$

You can see that the uncertainty in the momentum measurement, Δp is very large, since Δq in the denominator is very small. In fact, if the precision of the position measurement gets so great that the uncertainty Δq gets so small that it approaches zero, then Δp gets so large that it approaches infinity or becomes completely undefined.

To see if the uncertainty relations are more than just a mathematical result, Heisenberg considered a thought experiment.

From this thought experiment, and another for energy and time, Heisenberg concluded that the mutual uncertainties in position and momentum or energy and time really do exist. They are not the fault of the experimenter or the apparatus. They are a fundamental consequence of the quantum equations, built into every experiment in which quantum mechanics comes into play.

The Gamma-Ray Microscope

"If one wants to be clear about what is meant by 'position of an object,' for example of an electron . . . then one has to specify definite experiments by which the 'position of an electron' can be measured; otherwise this term has no meaning at all."

—Heisenberg, in uncertainty paper, 1927

Are the uncertainty relations that Heisenberg discovered in 1927 just the result of the equations used, or are they really built into every measurement? Heisenberg turned to a thought experiment, since he believed that all concepts in science require a definition based on actual, or possible, experimental observations.

Heisenberg pictured a microscope that obtains very high resolution by using high-energy gamma rays for illumination. No such microscope exists at present, but it could be constructed in principle. Heisenberg imagined using this microscope to see an electron and to measure its position. He found that the electron's position and momentum did indeed obey the uncertainty relation he had derived mathematically. Bohr pointed out some flaws in the experiment, but once these were corrected the demonstration was fully convincing.

In the corrected version of the thought experiment, a free electron sits directly beneath the center of the microscope's lens. The circular lens forms a cone of angle 2A from the electron. The electron is then illuminated from the left by gamma rays—high energy light which has the shortest wavelength. These yield the highest resolution, for according to a principle of wave optics, the microscope can resolve (that is, "see" or distinguish) objects to a size of Δx, which is related to the wavelength L of the gamma ray, by the expression:

$$\Delta x = L / (2\sin A)$$

However, in quantum mechanics, where a light wave can act like a particle, a gamma ray striking an electron gives it a kick. At the moment the light is diffracted by the electron into the microscope lens, the electron is thrust to the right. To be observed by the microscope, the gamma ray must be scattered into any angle within the cone of angle 2A. In quantum mechanics, the gamma ray carries momentum, as if it were a particle. The total momentum p is related to the wavelength by the formula

$$p = h / L, \text{ where h is Planck's constant.}$$

In the extreme case of diffraction of the gamma ray to the right edge of the lens, the total momentum in the x direction would be the sum of the electron's momentum p'_x in the x direction and the gamma ray's momentum in the x direction:

$$p'_x + (h \sin A) / L', \text{ where L' is the wave-}$$
length of the deflected gamma ray.

In the other extreme, the observed gamma ray recoils backward, just hitting the left edge of the lens. In this case, the total momentum in the x direction is:

$$p''_x - (h \sin A) / L''.$$

The final x momentum in each case must equal the initial x momentum, since momentum is never lost (it is *conserved*). Therefore, the final x momenta are equal to each other:

$$p'_x + (h \sin A) / L' = p''_x - (h \sin A) / L''$$

55

If A is small, then the wavelengths are approximately the same, $L' \sim L'' \sim L$. So we have

$$p''_x - p'_x = \Delta p_x \sim 2h \sin A / L$$

Since $\Delta x = L / (2 \sin A)$, we obtain a reciprocal relationship between the minimum uncertainty in the measured position, Δx, of the electron along the x axis and the uncertainty in its momentum, Δp_x, in the x direction:

$$\Delta p_x \sim h / \Delta x \quad \text{or} \quad \Delta p_x \, \Delta x \sim h.$$

For more than minimum uncertainty, the "greater than" sign may be added.

Except for the factor of 4π and an equal sign, this is Heisenberg's uncertainty relation for the simultaneous measurement of the position and momentum of an object.

Looking closer at this picture, modern physicists warn that it only hides an imaginary classical mechanical interaction one step deeper, in the collision between the photon and the electron. In fact Heisenberg's microscope, although it was a big help in developing and teaching the quantum theory, is not itself part of current understanding. The true quantum interaction, and the true uncertainty associated with it, cannot be demonstrated with any kind of picture that looks like everyday colliding objects. To get the actual result you must work through the formal mathematics that calculates probabilities for abstract quantum states.

Clever experiments on such interactions are still being done today. So far the experiments all confirm Heisenberg's conviction that there is no "real" microscopic classical collision at the bottom.

Over time, new interpretations of quantum theory arose, and it became clear that this revolutionary direction in science would change every observer's perspective of the physical world. As modern physicists entered the realm of abstract quantum thinking, they performed new experiments that would advance the field of quantum physics. Two important principles developed in the 1930s are entanglement and decoherence. Entanglement describes a reality in which subsystems of particles interact with each other, so therefore it is not possible to define a quantum state for an individual particle within a subsystem that belongs within a larger system. This principle was necessary to help explain experimental differences in the measurement of a single subsystem. Experimentally, an observer can only witness one state, but when not observed, a subsystem can exist in a variety of states. The idea that an unobserved system can exist in multiple states at the same time depending on its

entanglement with the environment is called decoherence. At the turn of the millennium, prominent quantum physicist Tony Leggett explained these two ideas and the experimental evidence used to prove them in this feature article, "Quantum Theory: Weird and Wonderful," from the December 1999 issue of Physics World. *—FH*

"Quantum Theory: Weird and Wonderful"
by Tony Leggett
Physics World, 1999

Quantum mechanics is a great deal more than a theory; it is a whole new way of looking at the world. When it was developed in the 1920s, quantum mechanics was viewed primarily as a way of making sense of the host of observations at the level of single electrons, atoms or molecules that could not be explained in terms of Newtonian mechanics and Maxwellian electrodynamics. Needless to say, it has been spectacularly successful in this task.

Around 75 years later, as we enter the new millennium, most physicists are confident that quantum mechanics is a fundamental and general description of the physical world. Indeed, serious attempts have been made to apply quantum ideas not merely to laboratory-scale inanimate matter but also, for example, to the workings of human consciousness and to the universe as a whole. Yet despite this confidence, the nagging questions that so vexed the founding fathers of quantum theory—and which many of them thought had finally been laid to rest after years of struggle—have refused to go away. Indeed, as we shall see, in many cases these questions have returned to haunt us in even more virulent forms. It is probably fair to say that, in the final years of this century, interest in the foundations of quantum mechanics is more widespread, and more intellectually respectable, than at any time since the invention of quantum theory.

I shall not have space here to discuss all the interesting technical advances of recent years, such as work on Zeno's paradox or the properties of "post-selected" states. Instead I will confine myself to two aspects of the quantum world-view that are particularly alien to classical physics: these are "entanglement" and "non-realization." These two topics are commonly associated with two famous paradoxes—the Einstein-Podolsky-Rosen (EPR) paradox and Schrödinger's cat.

Quantum mechanics is usually interpreted as describing the statistical properties of "ensembles" of similarly prepared systems, such as the neutrons in a neutron beam, rather than individual particles. The ensemble is described by a wavefunction that can be a function of both space and time. This wavefunction, which is complex, contains all the information that it is possible to know about the particles in the ensemble. The probability of a particle being at a particular position is given by the product of the wavefunction and its complex conjugate at that point. Energy, momentum and other quantities that can be measured in an experiment are represented by "operators," and their distributions can be calculated if the wavefunction is known. The indeterminacy or uncertainty principle means that it is impossible to assign definite values of certain pairs of variables, such as position and momentum, with arbitrary precision.

In quantum mechanics it is possible for a particle such as an electron to be in two or more different quantum states or "eigenstates" at the same time. These eigenstates correspond to definite, but different, values of a particular quantity such as momentum. However, when the momentum of a particular particle is measured, a definite value is always found—as experiment confirms! In the conventional or Copenhagen interpretation of quantum theory, the particle in question "collapses" into the eigenstate corresponding to that value, and remains in this state for future measurements. Or, to put it more accurately, those particles that, on measurement, are found to have a particular value of the momentum constitute a new ensemble for future measurements, with properties different from the original ensemble.

Entanglement and the EPR Paradox

Although the standard interpretation of quantum mechanics does not allow the particles in an ensemble to possess definite values of all measurable properties simultaneously, it can be shown that the experimental predictions made by the theory are nevertheless compatible with the simultaneous existence of these properties. (This view is contrary to a long-standing misconception that may have resulted from a misreading of some early work by John von Neumann.) However, the simultaneous existence of these properties does require that

certain non-standard, but not obviously unreasonable, assumptions are made about the effects of the measurement process.

The phenomenon of "entanglement" refers to the fact that the most general quantum description of an ensemble of systems in which each system is composed of two or more subsystems (such as pairs of electrons or photons) does not permit us to assign a *definite quantum state* to each of the individual subsystems. This turns out to have a much more dramatic consequence: if quantum mechanics gives the correct predictions for experiment and we are not prepared to relax very basic ideas about causality, then *independent of any theoretical interpretation*, the individual particles cannot be conceived of as possessing "properties" in their own right.

To introduce the idea of "entanglement," let us consider a single "spin-1/2" particle such as an electron. When the intrinsic angular momentum or "spin" of the particle is measured along any direction, the answer is always $+h$-bar/2 or $- h$-bar/2, where h-bar is the Planck constant divided by 2 pi. The most general pure quantum state of a spin-1/2 particle can be written as phi(n), where n is the unit vector in the direction along which the spin is guaranteed to be h-bar/2.

Now consider two distinguishable spin-1/2 particles: one possible pure state for this system would involve each particle being in a single-particle pure state. This is written formally as $phi_1(n_1)$ x $phi_2(n_2)$ where n_1 is the unit vector for particle 1 and n_2 is the unit vector for particle 2. In such a "product" state it is possible to view each particle as possessing properties in its own right.

Nothing really changes if we consider statistical mixtures of product states: the vectors n_1 and n_2 still exist for any given pair, but we may not know what these vectors are. For example, we may know that either particle 1 has its spin "up" and particle 2 has its spin "down," or vice versa, without knowing which of these two possible states the system is in. In such a case the experimental properties are still compatible with the idea that the particles "possess" individual properties but we do not know what these properties are.

However, we can also form "quantum superpositions" of product states and, as we shall see below, these so-called entangled states can have unique and counter-intuitive properties. The best-known example of an entangled state is that which corresponds to two spin-1/2 particles with a total spin of zero

$$\text{Upsilon}(1, 2) = (1/2^{1/2})[\{\text{phi}_1(n) \times \text{phi}_2(-n)\} - \{\text{phi}_1(-n) \times \text{phi}_2(n)\}]$$

where n is a unit vector in an arbitrary direction. If the spin of particle 1 along any axis is measured and found to be $+1/2$, then a measurement of the spin of particle 2 along the same axis is guaranteed to yield -1/2. This property, while surprising, is not the most important property of the entangled state. What is unique about the entangled state, by its very definition, is that it is impossible to assign a quantum state (even an unknown one!) to each of the particles individually. In other words, the individual particles cannot be regarded as possessing properties in their own right.

In 1964 the late John Bell showed that the possibility of entanglement had truly spectacular consequences. Bell considered an ensemble of pairs of spin-1/2 particles that have interacted in the past but are now so wide apart that they are space-like separated in the sense of special relativity (that is there is no time for a light signal to travel between them within the duration of the experiment). He then set out to find a description of the pairs, and their interactions with the measuring apparatus, which satisfied the three postulates that defined so-called "objective local" theories.

- Each particle is characterized by a set of variables. These variables might correspond to a quantum-mechanical wavefunction, but they do not have to. It is not excluded that the variables describing particles 1 and 2 have a strong statistical correlation.

- The statistical probability of a given outcome when the spin of particle 1 is measured along any axis is a function only of the properties of the relevant measuring apparatus and of the variables describing particle 1. In particular, the result is not physically affected either by the choice of measurement direction for particle 2, or by the outcome of that measurement. It is usually assumed that special relativity ensures, under appropriate experimental conditions, that this condition is satisfied.

- The properties of ensembles at a given time are determined only by the boundary conditions at earlier times: that is there is no "retrospective causality."

Bell's theorem effectively says that an objective local theory and quantum theory will give different predictions for the results of certain experiments. The first step is to prepare an ensemble of pairs of quantum particles in such a way that we believe the correct quantum-mechanical description is given by an entangled state. If we then perform the experiment under suitably ideal conditions, and verify the predictions of quantum mechanics, we have shown that *no theory of the objective local type can describe the physical world*. Note that this conclusion is valid even if quantum mechanics is not the correct theory.

The history of experiments to compare the predictions of quantum mechanics and objective local theories goes back almost 30 years, including a remarkable series of experiments by Alain Aspect and co-workers at the Institut d'Optique in Paris in the early 1980s. With some exceptions that we believe we understand, these experiments have confirmed the statistical predictions of quantum mechanics under conditions that, although not 100 % ideal, are sufficient to have convinced most physicists that nature cannot be described by any objective local theory.

Therefore, if one wishes to preserve the second and third postulates above—that is to preserve our usual conceptions about locality in special relativity and the "arrow of time"—we must then reject the first postulate. In other words we must accept that "isolated" physical subsystems need not possess "properties" in their own right. This conclusion, which again is independent of the validity of quantum mechanics, is highly counterintuitive.

In the last few years there have been a number of significant developments in this area. On the experimental side, Nicolas Gisin's group at the University of Geneva has confirmed the quantum predictions at spatial separations of greater than 10 kilometres. These experiments, and indeed all of the experiments performed so far in this area, rely on statistical averages over a number of measurements. However, Daniel Greenberger, Michael Horne and Anton Zeilinger (GHZ) have shown that if one considers three particles, rather than pairs of particles, it is possible, in principle, to discriminate between the predictions of quantum mechanics and objective local theories with a single measurement. In the GHZ approach there exists, under certain conditions, an experiment such that objective local theories predict that the outcome is 100 % "yes," while quantum mechanics predicts 100 % "no." Experiments along these lines are currently being developed.

Entanglement has also played an important role in the emerging field of quantum information. For example, a quantum computer could, in principle, exploit entanglement to perform certain computational tasks much faster than a conventional or classical computer.

Non-realization and Schrödinger's Cat

The second major element of the quantum world-view that is also completely counterintuitive to classical thinking is "non-realization" or, as it is more commonly called, the quantum measurement paradox. This is most famously demonstrated by Schrödinger's famous cat. In this thought experiment a cat is placed in a box, along with a radioactive atom that is connected to a vial containing a deadly poison. If the atom decays, it causes the vial to be smashed and the cat to be killed. When the box is closed we do not know if the atom has decayed or not. However, the atom is a quantum system, which means that it can be in both the decayed and non-decayed state at the same time. Therefore, the cat is also both dead and alive at the same time—which clearly does not happen in classical physics (or biology). However, when we open the box and look inside—that is when we make a measurement—the cat is either dead or alive.

Let us look at the situation more closely. Consider an ensemble of microscopic systems, such as electrons or photons, described by a state that is a quantum superposition of two orthogonal microstates, a and b. These microstates might be localized near one or other of the slits in a Young's double-slit interference experiment. We know that any measurement that we carry out to discriminate between the states will always reveal that each individual system in the ensemble to be either in state a or in state b. There is, however, overwhelming experimental evidence that if a measurement is not made, then the system remains in a quantum superposition of the two states.

If now we introduce a device that will amplify the microstate a to produce some state A of the macroworld, and amplify microstate b to produce a state B that is *macroscopically different* from A, then this same device will amplify the superposition of a and b to produce a corresponding superposition of the macroscopically distinct states A and B. Moreover, if we continue to interpret the concept of superposition at the macrolevel in the same way that we do at the microlevel, we are apparently forced to conclude that the relevant part of the macroscopic world does not realize a definite macroscopic state until it is observed! In other words the cat can be both dead and alive at the same time before we look at it.

A standard reaction to this argument, which can be traced back to Heisenberg, relies on an idea called "decoherence." In decoherence a macroscopic body interacts so strongly with its "environment" that its quantum state rapidly gets entangled with that of the environment. For example, the description of the cat by a superposition of "dead" and "alive" states is not realistic—we would certainly need, as a minimum, to "entangle" these states with the corresponding states of the vial containing the poison and so on. In such an entangled state quantum mechanics predicts that any measurement made on the system alone (i.e. with no corresponding measurement on the "environment") should give statistical results identical to those that would be obtained from a classical probabilistic mixture of the states A and B. In this classical state each system in the ensemble is either definitely in state A or definitely in state B, but we do not know which. As a consequence, it is argued, we can legitimately say that by the time the amplification of the microstates has reached the macrolevel, each individual system "really is" in one state or the other.

There is no doubt that the phenomenon of decoherence is real—it has a very firm theoretical basis, and has been confirmed in a very elegant series of quantum-optics experiments by Serge Haroche, Jean-Michel Raimond and co-workers at the Ecole Normale Supérieure in Paris. The two states in these experiments differed by about 10 photons, so they are not perhaps "macroscopically" distinct, but the principle is the same.

The question is whether invoking decoherence really solves the quantum measurement problem. A substantial minority of physicists (including the current author) feel that it does not, and this has led to several interesting developments in both theory and experiment over the last couple of decades.

Theoretical work in this area can be classified into two broad areas. The first covers work that accepts that, in principle, the formalism of quantum mechanics gives a complete description of the physical world at all levels, including the macroscopic and even the cosmological levels. Physicists who adopt this approach seek to re-interpret the formalism in such a way as to avoid or reduce the problems associated with "non-realization." Recent developments have included the "consistent-histories" interpretation and also its variants, the "Ithaca interpretation" of David Mermin, a vigorous revival of interest in the ideas of the late David Bohm, and various ideas in "quantum cosmology."

The second broad area covers "alternative" theories that, in general, do not preserve all the experimental predictions of standard quantum mechanics. These theories generally try to preserve the predictions of quantum mechanics at the atomic level, where the theory has been well tested, while providing a physical mechanism that allows a single definite macroscopic outcome to occur. Experimental tests of the alternative theories might be possible in the near future. The best-developed theory of this type is that advocated by Giancarlo Ghirardi, Alberto Rimini, Tullio Weber and Philip Pearle.

Over the last two decades it has become widely accepted that the traditional dogma—that is the belief that decoherence will always render macroscopic superpositions unobservable—may fail if the dissipative coupling between the system and the environment can be sufficiently controlled. Several experimental groups have therefore searched for evidence of macroscopic superpositions. The workhorse system for these experiments is a superconducting device that incorporates the Josephson effect, where it is not usually disputed that the states in question are indeed "macroscopically" distinct. These states differ in that 10^{15} or so electrons (about 1 microamp) are circulating in opposite directions: in one state the current is flowing in a clockwise direction, in the other the current is anticlockwise. What experimentalists look for in most of these experiments—and in related experiments on bio-magnetic molecules, mesoscopic devices and other systems—is evidence that quantum mechanics still gives reliable experimental predictions, even under conditions where the theory predicts superpositions of macroscopically distinct states. The evidence itself, however, is usually somewhat circumstantial in nature, involving phenomena such as tunnelling or resonance behaviour.

To date none of these experiments has produced any evidence for the breakdown of quantum mechanics. Indeed, in experiments where the parameters are well controlled, the agreement between experiment and the predictions of quantum theory has been quite satisfying. However, it is important to appreciate that no experiment to date has definitively excluded a "macrorealistic" view of the world in which a macroscopic object is in a definite macroscopic state at all times. The macrorealistic view is, needless to say, incompatible with the quantum picture. However, no one has shown so far that it makes experimental predictions that are incompatible with those of quantum theory for any experiments that have actually been performed. An experiment that, if successful, may be able to do this is currently being built by a group lead by Giordano Diambrini Palazzi of the University of Rome. If this experiment confirms the predictions of quantum mechanics, it will at the same time rule out the macrorealist view at the level of a Josephson device.

Quantum Outlooks

Whither quantum mechanics in the next millennium? We do not know, of course, but here are two reasonable guesses for the short term. First, irrespective of whether or not "quantum computation" becomes a reality, the exploitation of the weird properties of entangled states is only in its infancy. Second, experimental work related to the measurement paradox will become progressively more sophisticated and eventually advance into the areas of the brain and of consciousness.

This, of course, assumes that physicists will maintain their current faith in quantum mechanics as a complete description of physical reality. This is something on which I would personally bet only at even odds for the year 2100, and bet heavily against as regards the year 3000!

Leggett, Tony. "Quantum Theory: Weird and Wonderful" © *Physics World*, December 1999.

Computers are continually being upgraded. There is always a faster model with more memory and capabilities than previously imagined. Although computers operate based on quantum mechanical ideas, encoding information is still based on classical methods. A new type of computer is currently being developed by quantum physicists to adopt quantum methods for information processing. This is being done

with the hope that so-called quantum computers can simultaneously process information in multiple states, thus, exponentially increasing the capacity of a computer. By relating these states to each other, one can conceivably produce a multidimensional computer capable of communicating at multiple levels. Although it is difficult to imagine right now, given the pace of quantum technological advancement, the quantum computer might soon exist. In the next selection, one of today's best-known physicists, Anton Zeilinger, discusses the idea of quantum computing and how it might revolutionize communication in the future. —FH

From "Fundamentals of Quantum Information"
by Anton Zeilinger
Physics World, 1998

Ever since its invention in the 1920s, quantum physics has given rise to countless discussions about its meaning and about how to interpret the theory correctly. These discussions focus on issues like the Einstein-Podolsky-Rosen paradox, quantum non-locality and the role of measurement in quantum physics. In recent years, however, research into the very foundations of quantum mechanics has also led to a new field—quantum information technology. The use of quantum physics could revolutionize the way we communicate and process information.

The important new observation is that information is not independent of the physical laws used to store and processes it. Although modern computers rely on quantum mechanics to operate, the information itself is still encoded classically. A new approach is to treat information as a quantum concept and to ask what new insights can be gained by encoding this information in individual quantum systems. In other words, what happens when both the transmission and processing of information are governed by quantum laws?

The elementary quantity of information is the bit, which can take on one of two values—usually "0" and "1." Therefore, any physical realization of a bit needs a system with two well defined states, for example a switch where *off* represents "0" and *on* represents "1." A bit can also be represented by, for example, a certain voltage level in a logical circuit, a pit in a compact disc, a pulse of light in a glass fibre or the magnetization on a magnetic tape. In classical systems it is desirable to have the two states separated by a large energy barrier so that the value of the bit cannot change spontaneously.

Two-state systems are also used to encode information in quantum systems and it is traditional to call the two quantum states $|0\rangle$ and $|1\rangle$. The really novel feature of quantum information technology is that a quantum system can be in a superposition of different states. In a sense, the quantum bit can be in both the $|0\rangle$ state and the $|1\rangle$ state at the same time. This new feature has no parallel in classical information theory and in 1995 Ben Schuhmacher of Kenyon College in the US coined the word "qubit" to describe a quantum bit.

A well known example of quantum superposition is the double-slit experiment in which a beam of particles passes through a double slit and forms a wave-like interference pattern on a screen on the far side. The essential feature of quantum interference is that an interference pattern can be formed when there is only one particle in the apparatus at any one time. A necessary condition for quantum interference is that the experiment must be performed in such a way that there is no way of knowing, not even in principle, which of the two slits the particle passed through on its way to the screen.

Quantum interference can be explained by saying that the particle is in a superposition of the two experimental paths: passage through the upper slit⟩ and passage through the lower slit⟩. Similarly a quantum bit can be in a superposition of 0⟩ and 1⟩. Experiments in quantum information processing tend to use interferometers rather than double slits but the principle is the same. So far single-particle quantum interference has been observed with photons, electrons, neutrons and atoms.

Beyond the Bit

Any quantum mechanical system can be used as a qubit providing that it is possible to define one of its states as 0⟩ and another as 1⟩. From a practical point of view it is useful to have states that are clearly distinguishable. Furthermore, it is desirable to have states that have reasonably long lifetimes (on the scale of the experiment) so that the quantum information is not lost to the environment through decoherence. Photons, electrons, atoms, quantum dots and so on can all be used as qubits. It is also possible to use both internal states, such as the energy levels in an atom, and external states, such as the direction of propagation of a particle, as qubits.

The fact that quantum uncertainty comes into play in quantum information might seem to imply a loss of information. However, superposition is actually an asset, as can be seen when we consider systems of more than one qubit. What happens if we try to encode two bits of information onto two quantum particles? The straightforward approach would be to code one bit of information onto each qubit separately. This leads to four possibilities—$0\rangle_1\,0\rangle_2\,0\rangle_1\,1\rangle_2\,1\rangle_1\,0\rangle_2$ and $1\rangle_1\,1\rangle_2$— where $0\rangle_1\,1\rangle_2$ describes the situation where the first qubit has the value "0" and second qubit has the value "1," and so on. This approach corresponds exactly to a classical coding scheme in which these four possibilities would represent "00," "01," "10" and "11."

However, quantum mechanics offers a completely different way of encoding information onto two qubits. In principle it is possible to construct any superposition of the four states described above. A widely used choice of superpositions is the so-called Bell states. A key feature of these states is that they are "entangled." Entanglement describes correlations between quantum systems that are much stronger than any classical correlations.

As in classical coding, four different possibilities can be represented by the four Bell states, so the total amount of information that can be encoded onto the two qubits is still two bits. But now the information is encoded in such a way that neither of the two qubits carries any well defined information on its own: all of the information is encoded in their joint properties. Such entanglement is one of the really counterintuitive features of quantum mechanics and leads to most of the paradoxes and other mysteries of quantum mechanics.

It is evident that if we wish to encode more bits onto quantum systems, we have to use more qubits. This results in entanglements in higher dimensions, for example the so-called Greenberger-Horne-Zeilinger (GHZ) states, which are entangled superpositions of three qubits. In the state 1/2 (000⟩ + 111⟩), for instance, all three qubits are either "0" or "1" but none of the qubits has a well defined value on its own. Measurement of any one qubit will immediately result in the other two qubits attaining the same value.

Although it was shown that GHZ states lead to violent contradictions between a local realistic view of the world and quantum mechanics, it recently turned out that such states are significant in many quantum-information and quantum-computation schemes. For example, if we consider 000 and 111 to be the binary representations of "0" and "7," respectively, the GHZ state simply represents the coherent superposition $(1/\sqrt{2})(\text{"}0\text{"}\rangle + \text{"}7\text{"}\rangle)$. If a linear quantum computer has such a state as its input, it will process the superposition such that its output will be the superposition of the results for each input. This is what leads to the potentially massive parallelism of quantum computers.

It is evident that the basis chosen for encoding the quantum information, and the states chosen to represent

0⟩ and 1⟩, are both arbitrary. For example, let us assume that we have chosen polarization measured in a given direction as our basis, and that we have agreed to identify the horizontal polarization of a photon with "0" and its vertical polarization with "1." However, we could equally well rotate the plane in which we measure the polarization by 45°. The states in this new "conjugate" basis, 0′⟩ and 1′⟩, are related to the previous states by a 45° rotation in Hilbert space

$$0′⟩ = (1/\sqrt{\Delta 2})(0⟩ + 1⟩)$$
$$1′⟩ = (1/\sqrt{2})(0⟩ - 1⟩)$$

This rotation is known in information science as a Hadamard transformation. When spin is used to encode information in an experiment we can change the basis by a simple polarization rotation; when the directions of propagation are used, a beam splitter will suffice. It is important to note that conjugate bases cannot be used at the same time in an experiment, although the possibility of switching between various bases during an experiment—most notably between conjugate bases—is the foundation of the single-photon method of quantum cryptography.

Zeilinger, Anton. "Fundamentals of Quantum Information" © *Physics World*, March 1998.

3 Evolving Theories in Quantum Physics

Quantum physics can be broken up into two major subdomains: quantum mechanics and quantum field theory. Quantum mechanics describes the behavior of matter at an atomic level, whereas quantum field theory considers what goes on in a field or space. For example, quantum field theory addresses the emission of light when electrons jump from one energy state to another, and assumes that space is not empty but consists of a series of electromagnetic fields. Thus, understanding space is critical to understanding the forces of nature and has spurred an entire branch of quantum physics research. How do fields in space interact with each other? Quantum physicists are currently trying to answer these questions in order to establish a unified theory of space and time. Science writer Tom Siegfried relates quantum field theory to the study of space and time in the following excerpt from his book The Bit and the Pendulum. *—FH*

From *The Bit and the Pendulum*
by Tom Siegfried
2000

The Magical Mystery Theory

Space, as every *Star Trek* fan knows, is the final frontier.

It's the frontier of exploration. It's the frontier of discovery. It's the frontier of understanding the very nature of the universe. If Vince Lombardi were alive today, he would probably say that space is not really the final frontier—it's the only frontier.

Space (or "spacetime," to be more precise in the era of relativity) is where everything about reality comes together. At the frontiers of the scientific understanding of space and time, scientists have only a few clues, and no certainty, about how to answer the deepest questions. The standard physical ideas of space and time are not just written in books and accepted as established, but are topics of active theoretical interest these days. A lot of smart people are applying high-powered physics and math to figuring out what space and time are *really* like.

This research is producing some very new ideas and theoretical results that are not yet in any textbook. Some of them will never be, because some of them are surely wrong. It's just too soon to tell which of these ideas will lead the way to a new understanding of the universe. Nevertheless, a journey to the frontiers of spacetime research is sure to lead to new signs of the importance of information in the nature of reality and existence . . .

. . . Modern physics says space is full of different "fields." A particle is a knot in a field. A particle's identity depends on what kind of field it is a knot in.

But what's a field? Simply something sitting in space, inseparable from it, like the familiar electromagnetic field that broadcasts radio and TV and cellular phone signals. Photons are knots in the electromagnetic field, just as the matter particles known as quarks are knots in "quark" fields.

Fields make space more complicated than it seemed in the days of Newton and Leibniz. Someday, no doubt, it will turn out to be still more complicated. It remains to be explained, for example, how all the fields in space fit together—or in other words, how they are "unified." Einstein vainly sought a unified field theory that would have combined gravity and electromagnetism. Nowadays physicists speak of "grand unified theories" that combine the electromagnetic fields and nuclear force fields. Getting the gravitational field (that is, the underlying spacetime itself) to join in this unification has been difficult. This seems to be because the fields other than gravity are described by quantum mechanics. And marrying quantum mechanics and general relativity has been harder than negotiating peace in Bosnia.

This is all very perplexing, because quantum mechanics and general relativity are, in their separate domains, the most spectacularly successful theories in the history of science. They've explained a vast range of phenomena already known, and predicted bizarre new phenomena that have been confirmed by experiment and observation.

Quantum mechanics, for example, is at the heart of the "standard model" of particle physics, which succeeds in describing the fundamental particles of nature and the forces that guide them—except gravity. In physics, the standard model is the gold standard of theories.

"This theory is really amazing," says Nathan Seiberg, a theorist at the Institute for Advanced Study. "It's logically self consistent, so whenever we ask a question we get an unambiguous answer—it's always the same answer regardless of how we do the calculation. This sounds like a triviality but it's absolutely crucial . . . The second thing is that it agrees in a spectacular way with experiment . . . So this is more or less a complete story, and it's quite beautiful, it agrees with everything. But one thing is left out, and this is gravity . . . We can't put the two stories together."

So the situation as it stands is something like this. Matter is described in phenomenally precise detail by quantum mechanics. Relativity melded gravity, space, and matter. The frontier of understanding space today is the search for a theory of quantum gravity. On this much everybody agrees. And I think there's general agreement that finding a theory of quantum gravity will involve a deeper understanding of the nature of spacetime. The secrets of space seem tied up not only in the knots of the particles and forces, but also in the universe on the large scale. I think many of the important research issues in this regard can be summarized by discussing the efforts to answer three essential questions about space:

1. What is space like on very large scales?
2. What is space like on very small scales?
3. How many dimensions does space have?

Space on Large Scales

The question of what space is like on very large scales has been in the news a lot in the past few years—largely because the Hubble Space Telescope is such a news maker, and much of what it finds out is relevant to the big questions about the universe. Those questions include, of course, whether space on the large scale is curved so much that it will eventually collapse and we'll have a big crunch, or whether it will keep expanding forever. We don't know yet for sure, although at the moment the best bet is no crunch. In fact, the universe may very well be expanding at an ever accelerating rate. That evidence is not conclusive, though, and there could always be more surprises about what the universe is actually doing.

There are other questions about space on large scales that current astronomy is trying to answer. For example, how does the large-scale geometry of space affect things like the development of clusters of galaxies? Usually this is believed to be merely a question of general relativity. Relativity describes the universe on large scales, while quantum physics describes small scales. But there are some new analyses that suggest quantum effects might have a role to play on large-scale geometry.

Space on Small Scales

Space on very small scales, and I mean really very small scales, is a big preoccupation of physicists these days. They want to know what happens to the laws of physics when distances under consideration are much smaller than the smallest of subatomic particles. Einstein's equations do a good job of describing space, but at very tiny distances, about 10 to the minus 33 centimeters, problems develop. This distance is called the Planck length, and it's very, very small—enlarging something the size of the Planck length to the size of an atom would be like making a football stadium bigger than the entire universe.

So if you squeeze matter into a tiny space, it gets denser and denser, and space curls up very tightly. If you keep going and space curls up below the Planck length, Einstein's equations become helpless. They can no longer describe what's going on. This is what they say happens inside a black hole, at the center, where the density of matter is infinite, all the matter crushed into a single point called a singularity. There is no way to describe a singularity—space and time literally go away there—and so many physicists hope that singularities don't really exist.

The only way to figure out what's going on at distances so short, most experts believe, is to come up with a theory that combines quantum mechanics with general relativity to provide a complete quantum theory of gravity that will describe everything just fine. It's not an easy assignment. People working on this problem have come up with a lot of suggestions about what might happen at the Planck scale. Some suggest that there is just a shortest possible length. In fact, most attempts to combine quantum physics with gravity reach that conclusion. Just how that shortest possible length manifests itself physically is another question. Some theories suggest that if you try to cram more matter (or energy) into such a small space it doesn't curve the space up even tighter, it starts to make things bigger. Inside a black hole, what might happen is space that has been compressed down nearly out of existence bounces back and starts expanding, possibly making a whole new universe.

But there are other attempts to describe what space is like physically at these small scales, even without matter and energy around—in other words, a true vacuum. Quantum theory seems to require that it must be pretty turbulent down there. The vacuum of space is not a boring nothingness, but a lively place. Because of the uncertainty principle, you aren't allowed to say that there is zero energy in empty space. That would be too certain. Some energy can show up here and there for a short time; as long as it disappears later, the quantum rules are satisfied. Long ago, John Wheeler suggested, therefore, that spacetime is a "foam" with little tunnels popping into existence that lead from one part of space to another. These tunnels are called wormholes.

The study of wormholes has become quite elaborate in the decades since Wheeler's original suggestion.

Several physicists have proposed that space could be laced with wormholes that serve as passageways to entirely different universes. Stephen Hawking has been a major contributor to wormhole theory. But lately he has decided that space might not really behave this way. In fact, he has written papers suggesting that rather than tiny wormholes, tiny black holes pop into existence throughout space at the scale of the Planck length. These black holes are like minuscule bubbles that appear in pairs and then disappear. Hawking calls this idea the "quantum bubbles picture." He first had this idea in the late 1970s, before the wormhole picture came into vogue. But he couldn't work out the math for a black hole to appear out of nothingness and then disappear again, as the quantum rules ought to dictate. Eventually, though, he realized that the math works if the black holes appear in pairs.

During the time that a temporary (or "virtual") black hole exists, it could interact with other particles in the universe. For example, a particle might fall into a virtual black hole and then reemerge, but as a different particle, Hawking has suggested.

This would be another example of a black hole erasing information, causing worry among some physicists. But not Hawking. He thinks the black-hole-bubbles picture of small-scale space could have its advantages. In particular, he thinks it could lead to predictions of certain features of particle physics, like details of the strong nuclear force and the nature of the Higgs boson, a particle being sought today in powerful atom smashers. The bubble picture shows, in other words, how the consequences of space's structure on the smallest of scales could be observed in experiments within the reach of physical instrumentation. And that's just the sort of thing that a quantum gravity theory needs to be taken seriously . . .

Siegfried, Tom. *The Bit and the Pendulum: From Quantum Computing to M Theory—the New Physics of Information*. Reprinted with permission of John Wiley & Sons, Inc. © 2000.

The development of quantum field theory provided an acceptable resolution to the behavior of particles in space. However, one drawback to the theory is that it did not take into account the force of gravity. Gravitational behavior has been elegantly described by Einstein's theory of relativity in classical physics. Theoretical physicists are currently searching for a unifying theory of quantum gravity. Superstring theory was one of the first potential theories to address the problem of quantum gravity in the early 1970s, and hence received a great deal of publicity in the field. This theory describes particles as vibrating strings and postulates that different modes of vibration govern the existence of a particle type such as an electron, photon, or even a graviton, the particle that carries gravitational force. Michio Kaku and Jennifer Trainer Thompson tell the fascinating story of the superstring theory and its development in the

following selection from their book Beyond Einstein: Superstrings and the Quest for the Final Theory. *—FH*

From *Beyond Einstein: Superstrings and the Quest for the Final Theory*
by Michio Kaku and Jennifer Trainer Thompson
1997

The Birth of the Superstring Theory

The superstring theory has perhaps the weirdest history in the annals of science. Nowhere else do we find a theory that was proposed as the solution to the wrong problem, abandoned for over a decade, and then resurrected as a theory of the universe.

The superstring theory began in the 1960s, before the flourishing of the Yang-Mills theory and gauge symmetries, when the renormalization theory was still floundering as a theory bedeviled by infinities.

A backlash had developed against the renormalization theory, which seemed contrived and artificial. The opposing school of thought was led by Geoffrey Chew of the University of California at Berkeley, who proposed a new theory that was independent of elementary particles, Feynman diagrams, and the renormalization theory.

Instead of postulating a series of intricate rules detailing how certain elementary particles interact with other particles through Feynman diagrams, Chew's theory required only that the S-matrix (which mathematically describes the collisions of particles) be self-consistent. Chew's theory postulated that the S-matrix obeys a rigorous set of mathematical properties, and then assumed that these properties are so restrictive that only one solution was possible. This approach is often called the "bootstrap" approach, because one is literally picking oneself up by one's bootstraps (one begins with only a set of postulates, then theoretically derives the answer using only self-consistency).

Because Chew's approach was based entirely on the S-matrix, rather than on elementary particles or Feynman diagrams, the theory was called the "S-matrix theory" (not to be confused with the S-matrix itself, which all physicists use).

These two theories, quantum field theory and S-matrix theory, are based on different assumptions about the meaning of an "elementary particle." The quantum field theory is based on the assumption that all matter can be built from a small set of elementary particles, whereas the S-matrix theory is based on an infinite number of particles, with none of them elementary.

In retrospect, we see that the superstring theory combines the best features of the S-matrix theory and the quantum field theory, which in many ways are opposites.

The superstring theory resembles the quantum field theory because it is based on elementary units of matter. Instead of point particles, however, the superstring theory is based on strings that interact by breaking and reforming via Feynman-like diagrams. But the significant advantage that superstrings have over the quantum field theory is that renormalization is not required. All the loop diagrams at each level are

probably finite by themselves, requiring no artificial sleights of hand to remove the infinities.

Similarly, the superstring theory resembles the S-matrix theory in that it can accommodate an infinite number of "elementary particles." According to this theory, the infinite variety of particles found in nature are simply different resonances of the same string, with no particle any more fundamental than any other. The great advantage, however, that the superstring theory has over the S-matrix theory is that it is possible to calculate with the superstring theory and eventually get numbers for the S-matrix. (By contrast, the S-matrix theory is exceedingly difficult to calculate with and extract usable numbers.)

The superstring theory, then, incorporates the best features of both the S-matrix theory and the quantum field theory because it is based on a startlingly different physical picture.

The superstring theory, unlike the S-matrix theory or the quantum field theory, which were based on years of patient development, burst forth unexpectedly on the physics community in 1968. In fact, it was by sheer accident, and not a logical sequence of ideas, that the superstring idea was discovered.

Guessing the Answer

In 1968, when the S-matrix theory was still very much in vogue, two young physicists, Gabriele Veneziano and Mahiko Suzuki, each working independently at CERN, the nuclear research center outside Geneva, asked themselves a simple question: If the S-matrix is supposed to obey so many restrictive properties, then why not just try to guess the answer? They thumbed through voluminous tables of mathematical functions cataloged since the eighteenth century by mathematicians and stumbled upon the Beta function, a beautiful mathematical formula first written down by the Swiss mathematician Leonhard Euler in the 1800s. Much to their astonishment, upon examining the properties of the Beta function, they found that it automatically satisfied almost all of Chew's S-matrix postulates.

This was crazy. Was the solution to strong interaction physics simply a formula written down more than a hundred years earlier by a mathematician? Was it all so simple?

Making a major scientific discovery by randomly flipping through a math book had never happened before in the history of science. (Perhaps the fact that Veneziano and Suzuki were both too young to appreciate the odds against their random discovery helped them to find the Beta function. An older, more prejudiced physicist might have dismissed from the start the idea of finding the answer in an old math book.)

Euler's formula became an overnight sensation in the world of physics—the apparent victory of the S-matrix theory over the quantum field theory. Hundreds of papers were written trying to use the Beta function to fit the data pouring out of atom smashers. Many papers, in particular, were written to solve the last remaining postulate of Chew's that the Beta function did not obey: unitarity, or the conservation of probability.

Very rapidly, attempts were made to propose even more complex theories that would fit the data even better. Soon John Schwarz and French physicist Andre Neveu, both working at Princeton University at the time, and Pierre Ramond, then at the National Accelerator Laboratory near Chicago, proposed a theory that would include particles with "spin" (which eventually became the superstring theory).

As remarkable as the Beta function was, the nagging question remained: Were the marvelous properties of this formula strictly an accident, or did they arise from a deeper, more physical underlying structure? The answer was finally established in 1970, when Yoichiro Nambu of the University of Chicago showed that this marvelous Beta function was due to the properties of interacting strings. When this new approach was applied to the Neveu-Schwarz-Ramond theory, it became the present theory of the superstring . . .

Nambu's String

Nambu originally proposed the idea of the string to make some sense out of the chaos of the hundreds of hadrons being discovered in the nation's laboratories. Clearly, these hadrons could not be viewed as "fundamental" in any sense of the word. The disarray of strong interaction physics, Nambu thought, must be a reflection of some underlying structure.

One proposal, made years earlier by his colleague Yukawa, and others such as Heisenberg, assumed that elementary particles were not points at all but "blobs" that could pulsate and vibrate. Over the years, all efforts to build a quantum field theory based on blobs, membranes, and other geometric objects have failed. These theories eventually violated some physical principle, such as relativity (because if the blob was shaken at one point, the vibration could travel through the blob faster than the speed of light). They were only vaguely defined and extraordinarily difficult to use in any calculation.

Nambu's seminal idea was to assume that the hadron consisted of a vibrating string, with each mode of vibration corresponding to a separate particle. (The superstring theory would not violate relativity because vibrations along the string could travel only less than or at the speed of light.)

Think of our previous analogy of the violin string. Let's say that we are given a mysterious box that creates musical tones. If we knew nothing about music, we would first attempt to catalog the musical tones, giving them names, such as C, F, G, and so on. Our second strategy would be to discover relations among the notes, such as observing that they occur in groups of eight (octaves). From this we would be able to discover the laws of harmony. Last, we would try to postulate a "model" that would explain the harmonies and musical scale from a single principle, such as a vibrating violin string. Similarly, Nambu believed that the Beta function found by Veneziano and Suzuki could be explained by vibrating strings.

One problem remaining was to explain what happened when strings collided. Because each mode of the string represents a particle, understanding how strings collide allows us to calculate the S-matrix of ordinary particle interactions. Three physicists then working at the University of Wisconsin, Bunji Sakita, Keiji Kikkawa, and Miguel Virasoro, conjectured that the last remaining postulate (unitarity) of Chew's S-matrix could be satisfied in the same way as the renormalization theory solves this postulate: by adding loops. In other words, these physicists proposed to reintroduce Feynman diagrams for these strings. (At this point, many of the S-matrix theorists were dismayed. This heretical idea meant reintroducing loops and the renormalization theory, which they had banned from the S-matrix theory. This was too much for the purists in the S-matrix camp.)

Their proposal was finally completed by one of us (Michio) and a collaborator, Loh-Ping Yu, when they were graduate students at the University of California at Berkeley, and also by Claude Lovelace, then at CERN, and V. Alessandrini, a physicist from Argentina.

Since the birth of quantum physics, theoretical physicists have sought to unite quantum ideas with the rules of classical physics. This is an enormous challenge, since the two schools of thought are fundamentally different. Gravity is one force of classical physics that physicists are still striving to understand using quantum ideas.

Loop quantum gravity is one effort toward this goal. The theory of loop quantum gravity applies quantum ideas to space and time and proposes that space and time can also exist as discrete quantifiable states, just as the colors of a flame represent discrete energy states. The success of this theory required physicists to dismiss the assumption that space is smooth and continuous. In the following piece, theoretical physicist Lee Smolin explains his involvement in developing the theory of loop quantum gravity and describes the important applications of this theory to space and time within our cosmos. —FH

"Atoms of Space and Time"
by Lee Smolin
Scientific American, 2004

A little more than 100 years ago most people—and most scientists—thought of matter as continuous. Although since ancient times some philosophers and scientists had speculated that if matter were broken up into small enough bits, it might turn out to be made up of very tiny atoms, few thought the existence of atoms could ever be proved. Today we have imaged individual atoms and have studied the particles that compose them. The granularity of matter is old news.

In recent decades, physicists and mathematicians have asked if space is also made of discrete pieces. Is it continuous, as we learn in school, or is it more like a

piece of cloth, woven out of individual fibers? If we could probe to size scales that were small enough, would we see "atoms" of space, irreducible pieces of volume that cannot be broken into anything smaller? And what about time: Does nature change continuously, or does the world evolve in series of very tiny steps, acting more like a digital computer?

The past 16 years have seen great progress on these questions. A theory with the strange name of "loop quantum gravity" predicts that space and time are indeed made of discrete pieces. The picture revealed by calculations carried out within the framework of this theory is both simple and beautiful. The theory has deepened our understanding of puzzling phenomena having to do with black holes and the big bang. Best of all, it is testable; it makes predictions for experiments that can be done in the near future that will enable us to detect the atoms of space, if they are really there.

Quanta

My colleagues and I developed the theory of loop quantum gravity while struggling with a long-standing problem in physics: Is it possible to develop a quantum theory of gravity? To explain why this is an important question—and what it has to do with the granularity of space and time—I must first say a bit about quantum theory and the theory of gravity.

The theory of quantum mechanics was formulated in the first quarter of the 20th century, a development that was closely connected with the confirmation that matter is made of atoms. The equations of quantum mechanics require that certain quantities, such as the energy of an atom, can come only in specific, discrete units. Quantum theory successfully predicts the properties and behavior of atoms and the elementary particles and forces that compose them. No theory in the history of science has been more successful than quantum theory. It underlies our understanding of chemistry, atomic and subatomic physics, electronics and even biology.

In the same decades that quantum mechanics was being formulated, Albert Einstein constructed his general theory of relativity, which is a theory of gravity. In his theory, the gravitational force arises as a consequence of space and time (which together form "spacetime") being curved by the presence of matter. A loose analogy is that of a bowling ball placed on a rubber sheet along with a marble that is rolling around nearby. The balls could represent the sun and the earth, and the sheet is space. The bowling ball creates a deep indentation in the rubber sheet, and the slope of this indentation causes the marble to be deflected toward the larger ball, as if some force—gravity—were pulling it in that direction. Similarly, any piece of matter or concentration of energy distorts the geometry of spacetime, causing other particles and light rays to be deflected toward it, a phenomenon we call gravity.

Quantum theory and Einstein's theory of general relativity separately have each been fantastically well confirmed by experiment—but no experiment has explored the regime where both theories predict significant effects. The problem is that quantum effects are most prominent at small size scales, whereas general relativistic effects require large masses, so it takes extraordinary circumstances to combine both conditions.

Allied with this hole in the experimental data is a huge conceptual problem: Einstein's theory of general relativity is thoroughly classical, or nonquantum. For physics as a whole to be logically consistent, there has to be a theory that somehow unites quantum mechanics and general relativity. This long-sought-after theory is called quantum gravity. Because general relativity deals in the geometry of spacetime, a quantum theory of gravity will in addition be a quantum theory of spacetime.

Physicists have developed a considerable collection of mathematical procedures for turning a classical theory into a quantum one. Many theoretical physicists and mathematicians have worked on applying those standard techniques to general relativity. Early results were discouraging. Calculations carried out in the 1960s and 1970s seemed to show that quantum theory and general relativity could not be successfully combined. Consequently, something fundamentally new seemed to be required, such as additional postulates or principles not included in quantum theory and general relativity, or new particles or fields, or new entities of some kind. Perhaps with the right additions or a new mathematical structure, a quantumlike theory could be developed that would successfully approximate general relativity in the nonquantum regime. To avoid spoiling the successful predictions of quantum theory and general relativity, the exotica contained in the full theory would remain hidden from experiment except in the extraordinary circumstances where both quantum theory and general relativity are expected to have large effects. Many different approaches along these lines have been tried, with names such as twistor theory, noncommutative geometry and supergravity.

An approach that is very popular with physicists is string theory, which postulates that space has six or seven dimensions—all so far completely unobserved—in addition to the three that we are familiar with. String theory also predicts the existence of a great many new elementary particles and forces, for which there is so far no observable evidence. Some researchers believe that string theory is subsumed in a theory called M-theory [see "The Theory Formerly Known as Strings," by Michael J. Duff; SCIENTIFIC AMERICAN, February 1998], but unfortunately no precise definition of this conjectured theory has ever been given. Thus, many physicists and mathematicians are convinced that alternatives must be studied. Our loop quantum gravity theory is the best-developed alternative.

A Big Loophole

In the mid-1980s a few of us—including Abhay Ashtekar, now at Pennsylvania State University, Ted Jacobson of the University of Maryland and Carlo Rovelli, now at the University of the Mediterranean in Marseille—decided to reexamine the question of whether quantum mechanics could be combined consistently with general relativity using the standard techniques. We knew that the negative results from the

1970s had an important loophole. Those calculations assumed that the geometry of space is continuous and smooth, no matter how minutely we examine it, just as people had expected matter to be before the discovery of atoms. Some of our teachers and mentors had pointed out that if this assumption was wrong, the old calculations would not be reliable.

So we began searching for a way to do calculations without assuming that space is smooth and continuous. We insisted on not making any assumptions beyond the experimentally well tested principles of general relativity and quantum theory. In particular, we kept two key principles of general relativity at the heart of our calculations.

The first is known as background independence. This principle says that the geometry of spacetime is not fixed. Instead the geometry is an evolving, dynamical quantity. To find the geometry, one has to solve certain equations that include all the effects of matter and energy. Incidentally, string theory, as currently formulated, is not background independent; the equations describing the strings are set up in a predetermined classical (that is, nonquantum) spacetime.

The second principle, known by the imposing name diffeomorphism invariance, is closely related to background independence. This principle implies that, unlike theories prior to general relativity, one is free to choose any set of coordinates to map spacetime and express the equations. A point in spacetime is defined only by what physically happens at it, not by its location according to some special set of coordinates (no coordinates are special). Diffeomorphism invariance is very powerful and is of fundamental importance in general relativity.

By carefully combining these two principles with the standard techniques of quantum mechanics, we developed a mathematical language that allowed us to do a computation to determine whether space is continuous or discrete. That calculation revealed, to our delight, that space is quantized. We had laid the foundations of our theory of loop quantum gravity. The term "loop," by the way, arises from how some computations in the theory involve small loops marked out in spacetime.

The calculations have been redone by a number of physicists and mathematicians using a range of methods. Over the years since, the study of loop quantum gravity has grown into a healthy field of research, with many contributors around the world; our combined efforts give us confidence in the picture of spacetime I will describe.

Ours is a quantum theory of the structure of spacetime at the smallest size scales, so to explain how the theory works we need to consider what it predicts for a small region or volume. In dealing with quantum physics, it is essential to specify precisely what physical quantities are to be measured. To do so, we consider a region somewhere that is marked out by a boundary, B. The boundary may be defined by some matter, such as a cast-iron shell, or it may be defined by the geometry of spacetime itself, as in the event horizon of a black hole (a surface from within which even light cannot escape the black hole's gravitational clutches).

What happens if we measure the volume of the region? What are the possible outcomes allowed by both quantum theory and diffeomorphism invariance? If the geometry of space is continuous, the region could be of any size and the measurement result could be any positive real number; in particular, it could be as close as one wants to zero volume. But if the geometry is granular, then the measurement result can come from just a discrete set of numbers and it cannot be smaller than a certain minimum possible volume. The question is similar to asking how much energy electrons orbiting an atomic nucleus have. Classical mechanics predicts that an electron can possess any amount of energy, but quantum mechanics allows only specific energies (amounts in between those values do not occur). The difference is like that between the measure of something that flows continuously, like the 19th-century conception of water, and something that can be counted, like the atoms in that water.

The theory of loop quantum gravity predicts that space is like atoms: there is a discrete set of numbers that the volume-measuring experiment can return. Volume comes in distinct pieces. Another quantity we can measure is the area of the boundary B. Again, calculations using the theory return an unambiguous result: the area of the surface is discrete as well. In other words, space is not continuous. It comes only in specific quantum units of area and volume.

The possible values of volume and area are measured in units of a quantity called the Planck length. This length is related to the strength of gravity, the size of quanta and the speed of light. It measures the scale at which the geometry of space is no longer continuous. The Planck length is very small: 10^{-33} centimeter. The smallest possible nonzero area is about a square Planck length, or 10^{-66} cm^2. The smallest nonzero volume is approximately a cubic Planck length, 10^{-99} cm^3. Thus, the theory predicts that there are about 10^{99} atoms of volume in every cubic centimeter of space. The quantum of volume is so tiny that there are more such quanta in a cubic centimeter than there are cubic centimeters in the visible universe (10^{85}).

Spin Networks

What else does our theory tell us about spacetime? To start with, what do these quantum states of volume and area look like? Is space made up of a lot of little cubes or spheres? The answer is no—it's not that simple. Nevertheless, we can draw diagrams that represent the quantum states of volume and area. To those of us working in this field, these diagrams are beautiful because of their connection to an elegant branch of mathematics.

To see how these diagrams work, imagine that we have a lump of space shaped like a cube. In our diagrams, we would depict this cube as a dot, which represents the volume, with six lines sticking out, each of which represents one of the cube's faces. We have to write a number next to the dot to specify the quantity of volume, and on each line we write a number to specify the area of the face that the line represents.

Next, suppose we put a pyramid on top of the cube. These two polyhedra, which share a common face,

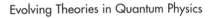
would be depicted as two dots (two volumes) connected by one of the lines (the face that joins the two volumes). The cube has five other faces (five lines sticking out), and the pyramid has four (four lines sticking out). It is clear how more complicated arrangements involving polyhedra other than cubes and pyramids could be depicted with these dot-and-line diagrams: each polyhedron of volume becomes a dot, or node, and each flat face of a polyhedron becomes a line, and the lines join the nodes in the way that the faces join the polyhedra together. Mathematicians call these line diagrams graphs.

Now in our theory, we throw away the drawings of polyhedra and just keep the graphs. The mathematics that describes the quantum states of volume and area gives us a set of rules for how the nodes and lines can be connected and what numbers can go where in a diagram. Every quantum state corresponds to one of these graphs, and every graph that obeys the rules corresponds to a quantum state. The graphs are a convenient shorthand for all the possible quantum states of space. (The mathematics and other details of the quantum states are too complicated to discuss here.)

The graphs are a better representation of the quantum states than the polyhedra are. In particular, some graphs connect in strange ways that cannot be converted into a tidy picture of polyhedra. For example, whenever space is curved, the polyhedra will not fit together properly in any drawing we could do, yet we can still easily draw a graph. Indeed, we can take a graph and from it calculate how much space is distorted. Because the distortion of space is what produces gravity, this is how the diagrams form a quantum theory of gravity.

For simplicity, we often draw the graphs in two dimensions, but it is better to imagine them filling three-dimensional space, because that is what they represent. Yet there is a conceptual trap here: the lines and nodes of a graph do not live at specific locations in space. Each graph is defined only by the way its pieces connect together and how they relate to well-defined boundaries such as boundary B. The continuous, three-dimensional space that you are imagining the graphs occupy *does not exist* as a separate entity. All that exist are the lines and nodes; they *are* space, and the way they connect defines the geometry of space.

These graphs are called spin networks because the numbers on them are related to quantities called spins. Roger Penrose of the University of Oxford first proposed in the early 1970s that spin networks might play a role in theories of quantum gravity. We were very pleased when we found, in 1994, that precise calculations confirmed his intuition. Readers familiar with Feynman diagrams should note that our spin networks are *not* Feynman diagrams, despite the superficial resemblance. Feynman diagrams represent quantum interactions between particles, which proceed from one quantum state to another. Our diagrams represent fixed quantum states of spatial volumes and areas.

The individual nodes and edges of the diagrams represent extremely small regions of space: a node is typically a volume of about one cubic Planck length, and a line is typically an area of about one square

Planck length. But in principle, nothing limits how big and complicated a spin network can be. If we could draw a detailed picture of the quantum state of our universe— the geometry of its space, as curved and warped by the gravitation of galaxies and black holes and everything else—it would be a gargantuan spin network of unimaginable complexity, with approximately 10^{184} nodes.

These spin networks describe the geometry of space. But what about all the matter and energy contained in that space? How do we represent particles and fields occupying positions and regions of space? Particles, such as electrons, correspond to certain types of nodes, which are represented by adding more labels on nodes. Fields, such as the electromagnetic field, are represented by additional labels on the lines of the graph. We represent particles and fields moving through space by these labels moving in discrete steps on the graphs.

Moves and Foams

Particles and fields are not the only things that move around. According to general relativity, the geometry of space changes in time. The bends and curves of space change as matter and energy move, and waves can pass through it like ripples on a lake [see "Ripples in Space and Time," by W. Wayt Gibbs; SCIENTIFIC AMERICAN, April 2002]. In loop quantum gravity, these processes are represented by changes in the graphs. They evolve in time by a succession of certain "moves" in which the connectivity of the graphs changes.

When physicists describe phenomena quantum-mechanically, they compute probabilities for different processes. We do the same when we apply loop quantum gravity theory to describe phenomena, whether it be particles and fields moving on the spin networks or the geometry of space itself evolving in time. In particular, Thomas Thiemann of the Perimeter Institute for Theoretical Physics in Waterloo, Ontario, has derived precise quantum probabilities for the spin network moves. With these the theory is completely specified: we have a well-defined procedure for computing the probability of any process that can occur in a world that obeys the rules of our theory. It remains only to do the computations and work out predictions for what could be observed in experiments of one kind or another.

Einstein's theories of special and general relativity join space and time together into the single, merged entity known as spacetime. The spin networks that represent space in loop quantum gravity theory accommodate the concept of spacetime by becoming what we call spin "foams." With the addition of another dimension—time—the lines of the spin networks grow to become two-dimensional surfaces, and the nodes grow to become lines. Transitions where the spin networks change (the moves discussed earlier) are now represented by nodes where the lines meet in the foam. The spin foam picture of spacetime was proposed by several people, including Carlo Rovelli, Mike Reisenberger (now of the University of Montevideo), John Barrett of the University of Nottingham, Louis Crane of Kansas State University, John Baez of the University of California at Riverside and Fotini Markopoulou of the Perimeter Institute for Theoretical Physics.

In the spacetime way of looking at things, a snapshot at a specific time is like a slice cutting across the spacetime. Taking such a slice through a spin foam produces a spin network. But it would be wrong to think of such a slice as moving continuously, like a smooth flow of time. Instead, just as space is defined by a spin network's discrete geometry, time is defined by the sequence of distinct moves that rearrange the network. In this way time also becomes discrete. Time flows not like a river but like the ticking of a clock, with "ticks" that are about as long as the Planck time: 10^{-43} second. Or, more precisely, time in our universe flows by the ticking of innumerable clocks—in a sense, at every location in the spin foam where a quantum "move" takes place, a clock at that location has ticked once.

Predictions and Tests

I have outlined what loop quantum gravity has to say about space and time at the Planck scale, but we cannot verify the theory directly by examining spacetime on that scale. It is too small. So how can we test the theory? An important test is whether one can derive classical general relativity as an approximation to loop quantum gravity. In other words, if the spin networks are like the threads woven into a piece of cloth, this is analogous to asking whether we can compute the right elastic properties for a sheet of the material by averaging over thousands of threads. Similarly, when averaged over many Planck lengths, do spin networks describe the geometry of space and its evolution in a way that agrees roughly with the "smooth cloth" of Einstein's classical theory? This is a difficult problem, but recently researchers have made progress for some cases, for certain configurations of the material, so to speak. For example, long-wavelength gravitational waves propagating on otherwise flat (uncurved) space can be described as excitations of specific quantum states described by the loop quantum gravity theory.

Another fruitful test is to see what loop quantum gravity has to say about one of the long-standing mysteries of gravitational physics and quantum theory: the thermodynamics of black holes, in particular their entropy, which is related to disorder. Physicists have computed predictions regarding black hole thermodynamics using a hybrid, approximate theory in which matter is treated quantum-mechanically but spacetime is not. A full quantum theory of gravity, such as loop quantum gravity, should be able to reproduce these predictions. Specifically, in the 1970s Jacob D. Bekenstein, now at the Hebrew University of Jerusalem, inferred that black holes must be ascribed an entropy proportional to their surface area [see "Information in a Holographic Universe," by Jacob D. Bekenstein; SCIENTIFIC AMERICAN, August 2003]. Shortly after, Stephen Hawking deduced that black holes, particularly small ones, must emit radiation. These predictions are among the greatest results of theoretical physics in the past 30 years.

To do the calculation in loop quantum gravity, we pick the boundary B to be the event horizon of a black hole. When we analyze the entropy of the relevant quantum states, we get *precisely* the prediction of Bekenstein. Similarly, the theory reproduces Hawking's

prediction of black hole radiation. In fact, it makes further predictions for the fine structure of Hawking radiation. If a microscopic black hole is ever observed, this prediction could be tested by studying the spectrum of radiation it emits. That may be far off in time, however, because we have no technology to make black holes, small or otherwise.

Indeed, any experimental test of loop quantum gravity would appear at first to be an immense technological challenge. The problem is that the characteristic effects described by the theory become significant only at the Planck scale, the very tiny size of the quanta of area and volume. The Planck scale is 16 orders of magnitude below the scale probed in the highest-energy particle accelerators currently planned (higher energy is needed to probe shorter, distance scales). Because we cannot reach the Planck scale with an accelerator, many people have held out little hope for the confirmation of quantum gravity theories.

In the past several years, however, a few imaginative young researchers have thought up new ways to test the predictions of loop quantum gravity that can be done now. These methods depend on the propagation of light across the universe. When light moves through a medium, its wavelength suffers some distortions, leading to effects such as bending in water and the separation of different wavelengths, or colors. These effects also occur for light and particles moving through the discrete space described by a spin network.

Unfortunately, the magnitude of the effects is proportional to the ratio of the Planck length to the wavelength. For visible light, this ratio is smaller than 10^{-28}; even for the most powerful cosmic rays ever observed, it is about one billionth. For any radiation we can observe, the effects of the granular structure of space are very small. What the young researchers spotted is that these effects accumulate when light travels a long distance. And we detect light and particles that come from billions of light years away, from events such as gamma-ray bursts [see "The Brightest Explosions in the Universe," by Neil Gehrels, Luigi Piro and Peter J. T. Leonard; SCIENTIFIC AMERICAN, December 2002].

A gamma-ray burst spews out photons in a range of energies in a very brief explosion. Calculations in loop quantum gravity, by Rodolfo Gambini of the University of the Republic in Uruguay, Jorge Pullin of Louisiana State University and others, predict that photons of different energies should travel at slightly different speeds and therefore arrive at slightly different times. We can look for this effect in data from satellite observations of gamma-ray bursts. So far the precision is about a factor of 1,000 below what is needed, but a new satellite observatory called GLAST, planned for 2006, will have the precision required.

The reader may ask if this result would mean that Einstein's theory of special relativity is wrong when it predicts a universal speed of light. Several people, including Giovanni Amelino-Camelia of the University of Rome "La Sapienza" and João Magueijo of Imperial College London, as well as myself, have developed modified versions of Einstein's theory that

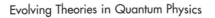

will accommodate high-energy photons traveling at different speeds. Our theories propose that the universal speed is the speed of very low energy photons or, equivalently, long-wavelength light.

Another possible effect of discrete spacetime involves very high energy cosmic rays. More than 30 years ago researchers predicted that cosmic-ray protons with an energy greater than 3×10^{19} electron volts would scatter off the cosmic microwave background that fills space and should therefore never reach the earth. Puzzlingly, a Japanese experiment called AGASA has detected more than 10 cosmic rays with an energy over this limit. But it turns out that the discrete structure of space can raise the energy required for the scattering reaction, allowing higher-energy cosmic-ray protons to reach the earth. If the AGASA observations hold up, and if no other explanation is found, then it may turn out that we have already detected the discreteness of space.

The Cosmos

In addition to making predictions about specific phenomena such as high-energy cosmic rays, loop quantum gravity has opened up a new window through which we can study deep cosmological questions such as those relating to the origins of our universe. We can use the theory to study the earliest moments of time just after the big bang. General relativity predicts that there was a first moment of time, but this conclusion ignores quantum physics (because general relativity is not a quantum theory). Recent loop quantum gravity calculations by

Martin Bojowald of the Max Planck Institute for Gravitational Physics in Golm, Germany, indicate that the big bang is actually a big bounce; before the bounce the universe was rapidly contracting. Theorists are now hard at work developing predictions for the early universe that may be testable in future cosmological observations. It is not impossible that in our lifetime we could see evidence of the time before the big bang.

A question of similar profundity concerns the cosmological constant—a positive or negative energy density that could permeate "empty" space. Recent observations of distant supernovae and the cosmic microwave background strongly indicate that this energy does exist and is positive, which accelerates the universe's expansion [see "The Quintessential Universe," by Jeremiah P. Ostriker and Paul J. Steinhardt; SCIENTIFIC AMERICAN, January 2001]. Loop quantum gravity has no trouble incorporating the positive energy density. This fact was demonstrated in 1990, when Hideo Kodama of Kyoto University wrote down equations describing an exact quantum state of a universe having a positive cosmological constant.

Many open questions remain to be answered in loop quantum gravity. Some are technical matters that need to be clarified. We would also like to understand how, if at all, special relativity must be modified at extremely high energies. So far our speculations on this topic are not solidly linked to loop quantum gravity calculations. In addition, we would like to know that classical general relativity is a good approximate description of the theory for distances much larger than the Planck length, in all circumstances. (At present we know only that the approximation is good for certain states that describe rather weak gravitational waves propagating on an otherwise flat spacetime.) Finally, we would like to understand whether or not loop quantum gravity has anything to say about unification: Are the different forces, including gravity, all aspects of a single, fundamental force? String theory is based on a particular idea about unification, but we also have ideas for achieving unification with loop quantum gravity.

Loop quantum gravity occupies a very important place in the development of physics. It is arguably the quantum theory of general relativity, because it makes no extra assumptions beyond the basic principles of quantum theory and relativity theory. The remarkable departure that it makes—proposing a discontinuous spacetime described by spin networks and spin foams—emerges from the mathematics of the theory itself, rather than being inserted as an ad hoc postulate.

Still, everything I have discussed is theoretical. It could be that in spite of all I have described here, space really is continuous, no matter how small the scale we probe. Then physicists would have to turn to more radical postulates, such as those of string theory. Because this is science, in the end experiment will decide. The good news is that the decision may come soon.

The paradox of quantum physics is that although it relies on abstract thought, it aims to bring order and understanding to the universe. Thus, there is an ongoing quest for the ultimate theory to incorporate and organize every thought and postulate that has been previously validated. The quest itself has progressed in multiple directions, and various theories are currently coexisting and coevolving. These theories exist as discrete states within the same system. This is the general idea of M-theory, which connects and provides a scaffold for other theories. M-theory has become especially useful as an approach to study black holes in space. This excerpt from the Cambridge Relativity and Gravitation Research Web site, which is administered by the Department of Applied Mathematics and Theoretical Physics at the University of Cambridge, provides a useful review of the evolving theories that led to M-theory. —FH

"M-Theory, the Theory Formerly Known as Strings"
by Carlos Herdeiro
Cambridge Relativity and Gravitation Research
Web Site, 1996

The Standard Model

In the standard model of particle physics, particles are considered to be points moving through space, tracing out a line called the World Line. To take into account the different interactions observed in Nature one has to provide particles with more degrees of freedom than only their position and velocity, such as mass, electric charge, color (which is the "charge" associated with the strong interaction) or spin.

The standard model was designed within a framework known as Quantum Field Theory (QFT), which gives us the tools to build theories consistent both with quantum mechanics and the special theory of relativity. With these tools, theories were built which describe with great success three of the four known interactions in Nature: Electromagnetism, and the Strong and Weak nuclear forces. Furthermore, a very successful unification between Electromagnetism and the Weak force was achieved (Electroweak Theory), and promising ideas put forward to try to include the Strong force. But unfortunately the fourth interaction, gravity, beautifully described by Einstein's General Relativity (GR), does not seem to fit into this scheme. Whenever one tries to apply the rules of QFT to GR one gets results which make no sense. For instance, the force between two gravitons (the particles that mediate gravitational interactions), becomes infinite and we do not know how to get rid of these infinities to get physically sensible results.

String Theory

In String Theory, the myriad of particle types is replaced by a single fundamental building block, a "string." These strings can be closed, like loops, or open, like a hair. As the string moves through time it traces out a tube or a sheet, according to whether it is closed or open. Furthermore, the string is free to vibrate, and different vibrational modes of the string represent the different particle types, since different modes are seen as different masses or spins.

One mode of vibration, or "note," makes the string appear as an electron, another as a photon. There is even a mode describing the graviton, the particle carrying the force of gravity, which is an important reason why String Theory has received so much attention. The point is that we can make sense of the interaction of two gravitons in String Theory in a way we could not in QFT. There are no infinities! And gravity is not something we put in by hand. It *has* to be there in a theory of strings. So, the first great achievement of String Theory was to give a consistent theory of quantum gravity, which resembles GR at macroscopic distances. Moreover String Theory also possesses the necessary degrees of freedom to describe the other interactions! At this point a great hope was created that String Theory would be able to unify all the known forces and particles together into a single "Theory of Everything."

From Strings to Superstrings

The particles known in nature are classified according to their spin into bosons (integer spin) or fermions (odd half integer spin). The former are the ones that carry forces, for example, the photon, which carries electromagnetic force, the gluon, which carries the strong nuclear force, and the graviton, which carries gravitational force. The latter make up the matter we are made of, like the electron or the quark. The original String Theory only described particles that were bosons, hence *Bosonic String Theory*. It did not describe fermions. So quarks and electrons, for instance, were not included in Bosonic String Theory.

By introducing *Supersymmetry* to Bosonic String Theory, we can obtain a new theory that describes both the forces and the matter which make up the Universe. This is the theory of *superstrings*. There are three different superstring theories which make sense, i.e. display no mathematical inconsistencies. In two of them the fundamental object is a closed string, while in the third, open strings are the building blocks. Furthermore, mixing the best features of the bosonic string and the superstring, we can create two other consistent theories of strings, Heterotic String Theories.

However, this abundance of theories of strings was a puzzle: If we are searching for the theory of everything, to have five of them is an embarrassment of riches! Fortunately, M-theory came to save us.

Extra Dimensions . . .

One of the most remarkable predictions of String Theory is that space-time has ten dimensions! At first sight, this may be seen as a reason to dismiss the theory altogether, as we obviously have only three dimensions of space and one of time. However, if we assume that six of these dimensions are curled up very tightly, then we may never be aware of their existence. Furthermore, having these so-called compact dimensions is very beneficial if String Theory is to describe a Theory of

Everything. The idea is that degrees of freedom like the electric charge of an electron will then arise simply as motion in the extra compact directions! The principle that compact dimensions may lead to unifying theories is not new, but dates from the 1920's, since the theory of Kaluza and Klein. In a sense, String Theory is the ultimate Kaluza-Klein theory.

For simplicity, it is usually assumed that the extra dimensions are wrapped up on six circles. For realistic results they are treated as being wrapped up on mathematical elaborations known as Calabi-Yau Manifolds and Orbifolds.

M-theory

Apart from the fact that instead of one there are five different, healthy theories of strings (three superstrings and two heterotic strings) there was another difficulty in studying these theories: we did not have tools to explore the theory over all possible values of the parameters in the theory. Each theory was like a large planet of which we only knew a small island somewhere on the planet. But over the last four years, techniques were developed to explore the theories more thoroughly, in other words, to travel around the seas in each of those planets and find new islands. And only then it was realized that those five string theories are actually islands on the same planet, not different ones! Thus there is an underlying theory of which all string theories are only different aspects. This was called M-theory. The M might stand for Mother of all theories or Mystery, because the planet we call M-theory is still largely unexplored.

There is still a third possibility for the M in M-theory. One of the islands that was found on the M-theory planet corresponds to a theory that lives not in 10 but in 11 dimensions. This seems to be telling us that M-theory should be viewed as an 11 dimensional theory that looks 10 dimensional at some points in its space of parameters. Such a theory could have as a fundamental object a Membrane, as opposed to a string. Like a drinking straw seen at a distance, the membranes would look like strings when we curl the 11th dimension into a small circle.

Black Holes in M-theory

Black Holes have been studied for many years as configurations of spacetime in General Relativity, corresponding to very strong gravitational fields. But since we cannot build a consistent quantum theory from GR, several puzzles were raised concerning the microscopic physics of black holes. One of the most intriguing was related to the entropy of Black Holes. In thermodynamics, entropy is the quantity that measures the number of states of a system that look the same. A very untidy room has a large entropy, since one can move something on the floor from one side of the room to the other and no one will notice because of the mess—they are equivalent states. In a very tidy room, if you change anything it will be noticeable, since everything has its own place. So we associate entropy to disorder. Black Holes have a huge disorder. However, no one knew what the states associated to the entropy of the Black Hole were. The last four years brought great excitement in this area. Similar techniques to the ones used to find the islands of M-theory, allowed us to explain exactly what states correspond to the disorder of some Black Holes, and to explain using fundamental theory the thermodynamic properties that had been deduced previously using less direct arguments.

Many other problems are still open, but the application of string theory to the study of Black Holes promises to be one of the most interesting topics for the next few years.

Cambridge Relativity & Gravitation Research Web site's public homepage: http://www.damtp.cam.ac.uk/user/gr/public/qg_ss.html.

The Second Quantum Revolution
Applications of Quantum Theory

Imagine what everyday life was like before the existence of cellular phones, television, computers, and other advanced technologies. That life would be the reality today without the discovery of quantum physics. Quantum ideas have permeated all aspects of modern life: understanding biomolecules, developing laser technology, increasing the capacity of computers, and exploring the cosmic universe. The application of quantum theory to technology is referred to as the second quantum revolution, or the quantum information revolution. This revolution took off in 1994, when quantum computers were first proposed. We are now in the midst of this revolution, and progress is increasing exponentially as new ideas are conceived based on the fundamental principles of quantum theory. Quantum computing physicists Jonathan P. Dowling and Gerard J. Milburn review the transformation of quantum theory into quantum technology in the following selection taken from the Philosophical Transactions of the Royal Society of London. —FH

From "Quantum Technology: The Second Quantum Revolution"
by Jonathan P. Dowling and Gerard J. Milburn
Philosophical Transactions of the Royal Society of London, 2003

1. Introduction

The *first quantum revolution* occurred at the last turn of the century, arising out of theoretical attempts to explain experiments on blackbody radiation. From that theory arose the fundamental idea of wave-particle duality—in particular the idea that matter particles sometimes behaved like waves, and that light waves sometimes acted like particles. This simple idea underlies nearly all of the scientific and technological breakthroughs associated with this *first quantum revolution*. Once you realize just how an electron acts like a wave, you now can understand the periodic table, chemical interactions, and electronic wave functions that underpin the electronic semiconductor physics. The latter technology drives the computer-chip industry and the so-called *Information Age*. On the other hand, the realization that a light wave must be treated as a particle gives to us the understanding we need to explain the photoelectric effect for constructing solar cells and photocopying machines. The concept of the photon is just what we need to understand the laser. By the end of this century, this first revolution of quantum mechanics has evolved into many of the core technologies underpinning modern society. However, there is a *second quantum revolution* coming—which will be responsible for most of the key physical technological advances in the 21st century.

Quantum technology allows us to organize and control the components of a complex system governed by the laws of quantum physics (Physics Survey Overview Committee 2001; Milburn 1996). This is in contrast to conventional technology which can be understood within the framework of classical mechanics. There are two imperatives driving quantum technology. The first is practical. The dominant trend in a century of technological innovation is miniaturization: to build devices on a smaller and smaller scale. Ultimately this will deliver devices at length-scales of nanometres and action scales approaching Planck's constant. At that point, design must be based on quantum principles. The second imperative is more fundamental. The principles of quantum mechanics appear to offer the promise of a vastly improved performance over what can be achieved within a classical framework.

The hallmark of this *second quantum revolution* is the realization that we humans are no longer passive observers of the quantum world that nature has given us. In the *first quantum revolution*, we used quantum mechanics to understand what already exists. We could explain the periodic table, but not design and build our own atoms. We could explain how metals and semiconductors behaved, but not do much to manipulate that behavior. The difference between science and technology is the ability to engineer your surroundings to your own ends, and not just explain them. In the *second quantum revolution*, we are now actively employing quantum mechanics to alter the quantum face of our physical world. We are transforming it into highly unnatural quantum states of our own design, for our own purpose. For example, in addition to explaining the periodic table, we can make new artificial atoms—quantum dots and excitons—which we can engineer to have electronic and optical properties of our own choosing. We can create states of quantum coherent or entangled matter and energy that are not likely to exist anywhere else in the Universe. These new man-made quantum states have novel properties of sensitivity and non-local correlation that have wide application to the development of computers, communications systems, sensors and compact metrological devices. Thus, although quantum mechanics as a science has matured completely, quantum engineering as a technology is now emerging on its own right. It is just a matter of being in the right place at the right time to take full advantage of these new developments.

Quantum Principles

The objective of quantum technology is to deliver useful devices and processes that are based on quantum principles, which include the following:

- Quantization (quantum size effect): the allowed energies of a tightly confined system of particles are restricted to a discrete set.

- Uncertainty principle: for every perfectly specified quantum state there is always at least one measurement, the results of which are completely certain, and simultaneously at least one measurement for which the results are largely random.

- Quantum superposition: if an event can be realized in two or more indistinguishable ways, the state of the system is a superposition of each way simultaneously.

- Tunnelling: the ability of a particle to be found in spatial regions from which classical mechanics would exclude it.

- Entanglement: the superposition principle applied to certain non-local correlations, if a correlation can be realized in two or more indistinguishable ways, the state of the system is a superposition of all such correlations simultaneously.

- Decoherence: what happens to quantum superpositions when an attempt is made to distinguish previously indistinguishable ways an event can be realized. It renders superpositions of probability amplitudes into superpositions of classical probabilities. Decoherence has no analogue in classical physics.

In this review we will encounter each of these principles applied in various current and emerging technologies. While we have understood them for many decades, only recently has it become possible to engineer devices according to these principles. In addition to fundamental principles of quantum mechanics, quantum technology will require a set of specific tools that are generic. These include: quantum metrology, quantum control, quantum communication and quantum computation.

The Tools of Quantum Technology

Successful technologies are predicated on precise engineering, which in turn requires high-precision measurement. Quantum technology will thus require us to develop a *quantum metrology*. It is well known that measurement in quantum mechanics requires a radical reappraisal of traditional measurement concepts. The modern description of measurement, in terms of quantum open systems (Paz & Zurek 2002), suffices to develop the principles required for measurement in a technological context. While many questions remain, it is clear that quantum mechanics enables new types of high-precision measurement (Berquist *et al.* 2001).

No complex technology can function without incorporating *control systems*: feedback, feed-forward, error correction, etc. Control systems take as input a measurement record, perform complex signal analysis in the presence of noise, and use the information gained to adapt the dynamics of the system or measurement in some way. Some years ago a simple theory of quantum control and feedback (Wiseman & Milburn

1993; Wiseman & Milburn 2002) was developed, which indicates that classical control theory is inadequate. The development of the general principles of quantum control theory is an essential task for a future quantum technology (Doherty *et al.* 2001).

The recent discovery of *quantum communication* protocols (Brassard 2001) that are more powerful than can be achieved classically suggests new ways for components of a large complex system to be interconnected. Quantum communication technologies require new principles of operation. A *quantum Internet* based on quantum optical channels, for example, would require new protocols for communication (e.g. distributed quantum computing, quantum packet switching) and might incorporate quantum key distribution and error correction as fundamental components. Already it is clear that there is a need to develop an understanding of quantum communication complexity.

Quantum mechanics enables exponentially more efficient algorithms than can be implemented on a classical computer. (Milburn 1998; Nielsen & Chuang 2000). This discovery has led to the explosive growth of the field of *quantum computation*. Building a quantum computer is the greatest challenge for a future quantum technology, requiring the ability to manipulate quantum-entangled states for millions of sub-components. Such a technology will necessarily incorporate the previous three quantum applications for read-out (*quantum metrology*), error correction (*quantum control*), and interconnects (*quantum communication*). A systematic development of the principles of measurement, control, and communication in a quantum world will facilitate the task of building a quantum computer.

2. Quantum Technologies

Quantum Information Technology

Quantum information technology is the advance guard of the second quantum revolution and has, in part, its origins in what were once little-known and little understood "second-order" effects predicted by the quantum theory. The earliest recognition of these effects came in 1935 in a famous paper by Einstein, Podolsky, and Rosen (EPR), who pointed out that certain carefully prepared quantum systems have non-local, entangled, non-classical correlations between them (Einstein *et al.* 1935). These EPR correlations are not just a manifestation of the usual wave-particle duality, but rather they are a new type of higher-level quantum effect that manifests itself only in precisely engineered man-made quantum architectures. For this reason, the first physical determination of these non-local EPR effects did not occur until around 1980, in small table-top quantum optical experiments by Clauser & Shimony (1978) and also Aspect *et al.* (1982).

From 1980 until 1994, the theory and experiments on non-local quantum correlations remained an obscure branch of the foundations of quantum mechanics. However, all that changed with two breakthroughs in 1994, when two critical events took place that began the quantum information revolution. The first was the experimental demonstration, by a group at the British

Defence Evaluation and Research Agency, that non-local photon correlations could be used to make an unbreakable quantum cryptographic key distribution system over 4 km of optical fiber (Tapster *et al.* 1994). The second was the theoretical exposition by Shor that a quantum computer, by harnessing these delicate non-local quantum entanglements, could provide an exponential speed up in computational power for some intractable numerical problems (Shor 1994, 1997; Ekert & Jozsa 1996). Thus, in 1994 the world learned that quantum entanglement was an important technological tool and not just a curiosity. Thence, the rapidly growing fields of quantum information theory and quantum computing were born (Milburn 1998; Nielsen & Chuang 2000).

These research areas provide the theoretical underpinnings that bind the other applied quantum technologies together; providing an over-arching theoretical and interpretive framework connecting advances in one topic to those in another. There is now a worldwide effort to build simple quantum information processors. These devices are a long way from a general purpose quantum computer but may be very powerful special purpose machines (such as a factoring engine for code breaking). Even that outcome is a decade or more away as we need to learn how to engineer entanglement on a scale of hundreds of particles. Many physical systems have been suggested for building a quantum computer, including: NMR, ion traps, cavity QED, quantum dots, superconducting circuits, and optical systems. Each particular system will require enormous advances in their respective fields and thus hasten the development of many different quantum technologies.

References

Aspect, A., Grangier, P. & Roger, G. 1982. Experimental realization of Einstein–Podolsky–Rosen–Bohm gedanken experiment: a new violation of Bell inequalities. *Phys. Rev. Lett.* **49**, 91–94.

Bergquist, J. C., Jefferts, S. & Wineland, D.J. 2001. Time measurement at the millennium. *Phys. Today* **54**, 37–44.

Brassard, G. 2001. Quantum communication complexity (a survey). *In Decoherence and its implications in quantum computing and information transfer. Proc NATO Advanced Research Workshop, Mykonos, Greece, 25–30 June 2000* (ed. A. Gonis & P. E. A. Turchi), pp. 199–210. Amsterdam: IOS Press.

Clauser, J. F. & Shimony, A. 1978. Bell's theorem: experimental tests and implications. *Rep. Prog. Phys.* **41**, 1881–1927.

Doherty, A. C., Habib, S., Jacobs, K., Mabuchi, H. & Tan, S.M. 2001. Quantum feedback control and classical control theory. *Phys. Rev.* A **62**, 012105.

Einstein, A., Podolsky, B. & Rosen, N. 1935. Can quantum-mechanical description of physical reality be considered complete? *Phys. Rev.* **47**, 777–780.

Ekert, A. & Jozsa, R. 1996. Quantum computation and Shor's factoring algorithm. *Rev. Mod. Phys.* **68**, 733–753.

Milburn, G. J. 1996. *Quantum technology.* Sydney: Allen &Unwin.

Milburn, G. J. 1998. *The Feynman processor: quantum entanglement and the computing evolution.* Frontiers of Science. Sydney: Perseus Books.

Milburn, G. J. & Wiseman, H. 2002. *Quantum measurement and control.* Cambridge University Press.

Nielsen, M. & Chuang, I. 2000. *Quantum information and computation.* Cambridge University Press.

Paz, J. P. & Zurek, W. H. 2002. *Environment induced decoherence and the transition from quantum to classical.* Lecture Notes in Physics, vol. 587. Springer.

Physics Survey Overview Committee. 2001. *Physics in a new era.* Report of the US National Research Council Board on Physics and Astronomy, Division of Engineering and Physical Science.

Shor, P. W. 1994. *Proc. 35th Annual Symp. on Foundations of Computer Science* (ed. S. Goldwasser). Los Alamitos, CA: IEEE Computer Society Press.

Shor, P. W. 1997. Polynomial-time algorithms for prime factorization and discrete logarithms on a quantum computer. *SIAM J. Computing* **26**, 1484–1509.

Tapster, P., Rarity, J. G. & Owens, P. C. M. 1994. Violation of Bell inequality over 4 km of optical-fiber. *Phys. Rev. Lett.* **73**, 1923–1926.

Wiseman, H. M. & Milburn, G. J. 1993. Quantum theory of optical feedback via homodyne detection. *Phys. Rev. Lett.* 70, 548–551.

Dowling, J. P., and G. J. Milburn. "Quantum Technology: The Second Revolution." *Philosophical Transactions of the Royal Society of London, A* (2003).

One of the most important developments in quantum technology was the elucidation of the theory of superconductivity in 1957 by physicists John Bardeen, Leon Cooper, and Robert Schrieffer. This theory described the conduction of electricity without resistance and loss of energy that occurs in normal metals. Superconductors require electrons to be paired such that they do not repel each other. By traveling in pairs, the electrons are organized and not scattered as they travel down the material. This creates a supercurrent that eliminates resistance and creates powerful magnetic fields. The phenomenon of superconductivity has been harnessed to create useful tools such as magnetic resonance imaging (MRI). Brain imaging with MRI machines has aided doctors in a variety of diagnostic procedures and helped researchers understand the mind. The following piece gives insight into the fascinating applications of superconductivity and ponders the future use of superconductors in the advancement of technology. —FH

"Superconductivity: A Macroscopic Quantum Phenomenon"
by John Clarke
Beam Line, 2000

In the Netherlands in 1911, about a decade after the discovery of quantum theory but more than a decade before the introduction of quantum mechanics, Heike Kamerlingh Onnes discovered superconductivity. This discovery came three years after he succeeded in liquefying helium, thus acquiring the refrigeration technique necessary to reach temperatures of a few degrees above absolute zero. The key feature of a superconductor is that it can carry an electrical current forever with no decay. The microscopic origin of superconductivity proved to be elusive, however, and it was not until 1957, after 30 years of quantum mechanics, that John Bardeen, Leon Cooper, and Robert Schrieffer elucidated their famous theory of superconductivity which held that the loss of electrical resistance was the result of electron "pairing."

In a normal metal, electrical currents are carried by electrons which are scattered, giving rise to resistance. Since each carry a negative electric charge, they repel each other. In a superconductor, on the other hand, there is an attractive force between electrons of opposite momentum and opposite spin that overcomes this repulsion, enabling them to form pairs. These pairs are able to move through the material effectively without being scattered, and thus carry a supercurrent with no energy loss. Each pair can be described by a quantum mechanical "wave function." The remarkable property of the superconductor is that all electron pairs have the same wave function, thus forming a macroscopic quantum state with a phase coherence extending throughout the material.

There are two types of superconductors. In 1957, Alexei Abrikosov showed that above a certain threshold magnetic field, type II superconductors admit field in the form of vortices. Each vortex contains one quantum of magnetic flux (product of magnetic field and area). Because supercurrents can flow around the vortices, these materials remain superconducting to vastly higher magnetic fields than their type I counterparts. Type II materials are the enabling technology for high-field magnets.

Shortly afterwards came a succession of events that heralded the age of superconducting electronics. In 1960, Ivar Giaever discovered the tunneling of electrons through an insulating barrier separating two thin superconducting films. If the insulator is sufficiently thin, electrons will "tunnel" through it. Building on this notion, in 1962 Brian Josephson predicted that electron pairs could tunnel through a barrier between two superconductors, giving the junction weak superconducting properties. Sure enough, this quantum mechanical phenomenon, called the "Josephson effect," was observed shortly afterwards at Bell Telephone Laboratories.

Between the two tunneling discoveries, in 1961, there occurred another discovery that was to have profound implications: flux quantization. Because supercurrents are lossless, they can flow indefinitely around a superconducting loop, thereby maintaining a permanent magnetic field. This is the principle of the high-field magnet. However, the magnetic flux threading the ring cannot take arbitrary values, but instead is quantized in units of the flux quantum. The superconductor consequently mimics familiar quantum effects in atoms but does so on a macroscopic scale.

For most of the century, superconductivity was a phenomenon of liquid helium temperatures; a compound of niobium and germanium had the highest transition temperature, about 23 K. In 1986, however, Alex Mueller and Georg Bednorz staggered the physics world with their announcement of superconductivity at 30 K in a layered oxide of the elements lanthanum, calcium, copper, and oxygen. Their amazing breakthrough unleashed a worldwide race to discover materials with higher critical temperatures. Shortly afterwards, the discovery of superconductivity in a compound of yttrium, barium, copper, and oxygen at 90 K ushered in the new age of superconductors for which liquid nitrogen, boiling at 77 K, could be used as the cryogen. Today the highest transition temperature, in a mercury-based oxide, is about 133 K.

Why do these new materials have such high transition temperatures? Amazingly, some 13 years after their discovery, nobody knows! While it is clear that hole pairs carry the supercurrent, it is unclear what glues them together. The nature of the pairing mechanism in high-temperature superconductors remains one of the great physics challenges of the new millennium.

Large-Scale Applications

Copper-clad wire made from an alloy of niobium and titanium is the conductor of choice for magnetic fields up to 10 tesla. Magnets made of this wire are widely used in experiments ranging from high-field nuclear magnetic resonance to the study of how electrons behave in the presence of extremely high magnetic fields. The largest scale applications of superconducting wire, however, are in magnets for particle accelerators and magnetic resonance imaging (MRI). Other prototype applications include cables for power transmission, large inductors for energy storage, power generators and electric motors, magnetically levitated trains, and bearings for energy-storing flywheels. Higher magnetic fields can be achieved with other niobium alloys involving tin or aluminum, but these materials are brittle and require special handling. Much progress has been made with multifilamentary wires consisting of the high temperature superconductor bismuth-strontium-calcium- copper-oxide sheathed in silver. Such wire is now available in lengths of several hundred meters and has been used in demonstrations such as electric motors and power transmission. At 4.2 K this wire remains superconducting to higher magnetic fields than the niobium alloys, so that it can be used as an insert coil to boost the magnetic field produced by low-temperature magnets.

The world's most powerful particle accelerators rely on magnets wound with superconducting cables. This cable contains 20–40 niobium-titanium wires in

parallel, each containing 5,000–10,000 filaments capable of carrying 10,000 amperes.

The first superconducting accelerator to be built was the Tevatron at Fermi National Accelerator Laboratory in 1984. This 1 TeV machine incorporates 800 superconducting magnets. Other superconducting accelerators include HERA at the Deutsches Elektronen Synchrotron in Germany, the Relativistic Heavy Ion Collider nearing completion at Brookhaven National Laboratory in New York, and the Large Hadron Collider (LHC) which is being built in the tunnel of the existing Large Electron Positron ring at CERN in Switzerland. The LHC, scheduled for completion in 2005, is designed for 14 TeV collision energy and, with quadrupole and corrector magnets, will involve more than 8,000 superconducting magnets. The dipole field is 8.4 tesla. The ill-fated Superconducting Super Collider was designed for 40 TeV and was to have involved 4,000 superconducting dipole magnets. At the other end of the size and energy scale is Helios 1, a 0.7 GeV synchrotron X-ray source for lithography operating at IBM. From these examples, it becomes clear that the demanding requirements of accelerators have been a major driving force behind the development of superconducting magnets. Their crucial advantage is that they dissipate very little power compared with conventional magnets.

Millions of people around the world have been surrounded by a superconducting magnet while having a magnetic resonance image (MRI) taken of themselves. Thousands of MRI machines are in everyday use, each containing tens of kilometers of superconducting wire wound into a persistent-current solenoid. The magnet is cooled either by liquid helium or by a cryocooler. Once the current has been stored in the superconducting coil, the magnetic field is very stable, decaying by as little as a part per million in a year.

Conventional MRI relies on the fact that protons possess spin and thus a magnetic moment. In the MRI machine, a radiofrequency pulse of magnetic field induces protons in the patient to precess about the direction of the static magnetic field supplied by the superconduting magnet. For the workhorse machines with a field of 1.5 T, the precessional frequency, which is precisely proportional to the field, is about 64 MHz. These precessing magnetic moments induce a radiofrequency voltage in a receiver coil that is amplified and stored for subsequent analysis. If the magnetic field were uniform, all the protons would precess at the same frequency. The key to obtaining an image is the use of magnetic field gradients to define a "voxel," a volume typically 3 mm across. One distinguishes structure by virtue of the fact that, for example, fat and muscle and grey and white matter produce different signal strengths.

MRI has become a clinical tool of great importance and is used in a wide variety of modes. The development of functional magnetic resonant imaging enables one to locate some sites in the brain that are involved in body function or thought. During brain activity, there is a rapid, momentary increase in blood flow to a specific site, thereby increasing the local oxygen concentration.

In turn, the presence of the oxygen modifies the local MRI signal relative to that of the surrounding tissue, enabling one to pinpoint the neural activity. Applications of this technique include mapping the brain and pre-operative surgical planning.

Small-Scale Applications

At the lower end of the size scale (less than a millimeter) are extremely sensitive devices used to measure magnetic fields. Called "SQUIDS" for superconducting quantum interference devices, they are the most sensitive type of detector known to science, and can turn a change in a magnetic field, something very hard to measure, into a change in voltage, something easy to measure. The dc SQUID consists of two junctions connected in parallel to form a superconducting loop. In the presence of an appropriate current, a voltage is developed across the junctions. If one changes the magnetic field threading the loop, this voltage oscillates back and forth with a period of one flux quantum. One detects a change in magnetic field by measuring the resulting change in voltage across the SQUID using conventional electronics. In essence, the SQUID is a flux-to-voltage transducer.

SQUIDs are fabricated from thin films using photolithographic techniques to pattern them on a silicon wafer. In the usual design, they consist of a square washer of niobium containing a slit on either side of which is a tunnel junction. The upper electrodes of the junctions are connected to close the loop. A spiral niobium coil with typically 50 turns is deposited over the top of the washer, separated from it by an insulating layer. A current passed through the coil efficiently couples flux to the SQUID. A typical SQUID can detect one part per million of a flux quantum, and it is this remarkable sensitivity that makes possible a host of applications.

Generally, SQUIDs are coupled to auxiliary components, such as a superconducting loop connected to the input terminals of the coil to form a "flux transformer." When we apply a magnetic field to this loop, flux quantization induces a supercurrent in the transformer and hence a flux in the SQUID. The flux transformer functions as a sort of "hearing aid," enabling one to detect a magnetic field as much as eleven orders of magnitude below that of the magnetic field of the earth. If, instead, we connect a resistance in series with the SQUID coil, we create a voltmeter that readily achieves a voltage noise six orders of magnitude below that of semiconductor amplifiers.

It is likely that most SQUIDs ever made are used for studies of the human brain. Commercially available systems contain as many as 306 sensors arranged in a helmet containing liquid helium that fits around the back, top, and sides of the patient's skull. This completely non-invasive technique enables one to detect the tiny magnetic fields produced by thousands of neurons firing in concert. Although the fields outside the head are quite large by SQUID standards, they are minuscule compared with environmental magnetic noise—cars, elevators, television stations.

To eliminate these noise sources, the patient is usually enclosed in a magnetically-shielded room. In addition, the flux transformers are generally configured as spatial gradiometers that discriminate against distant noise sources in favor of nearby signal sources. Computer processing of the signals from the array of SQUIDs enables one to locate the source to within 2–3 mm.

There are two broad classes of signal: stimulated, the brain's response to an external stimulus; and spontaneous, self-generated by the brain. An example of the first is pre-surgical screening of brain tumors. By applying stimuli, one can map out the brain function in the vicinity of the tumor, thereby enabling the surgeon to choose the least damaging path to remove it. An example of spontaneous signals is their use to identify the location of epileptic foci. The fast temporal response of the SQUID, a few milliseconds, enables one to demonstrate that some patients have two foci, one of which stimulates the other. By locating the epileptic focus non-invasively before surgery, one can make an informed decision about the type of treatment. Research is also under way on other disorders, including Alzheimer's and Parkinson's diseases, and recovery from stroke.

There are many other applications of low-temperature SQUIDs, ranging from the ultra-sensitive detection of nuclear magnetic resonance to searches for magnetic monopoles and studies of the reversal of the Earth's magnetic field in ancient times. A recent example of the SQUID's versatility is the proposal to use it as a high-frequency amplifier in an upgraded axion detector at Lawrence Livermore National Laboratory. The axion is a candidate particle for the cold dark matter that constitutes a large fraction of the mass of the Universe.

With the advent of high-temperature superconductivity, many groups around the world chose the SQUID to develop their thin-film technology. Yttrium-barium-copper-oxygen dc SQUIDs operating in liquid nitrogen achieve a magnetic field sensitivity within a factor of 3–5 of their liquid-helium cooled cousins. High-temperature SQUIDs find novel applications in which the potential economy and convenience of cooling with liquid nitrogen or a cryocooler are strong incentives. Much effort has been expended to develop them for magnetocardiography (MCG) in an unshielded environment. The magnetic signal from the heart is easily detected by a SQUID in a shielded enclosure. However, to reduce the system cost and to make MCG more broadly available, it is essential to eliminate the shielded room. This challenge can be met by taking spatial derivatives, often with a combination of hardware and software, to reduce external interference. What advantages does MCG offer over conventional electrocardiography? One potentially important application is the detection of ischemia (localized tissue anemia); another is to locate the site of an arrhythmia. Although extensive clinical trials would be required to demonstrate its efficacy, MCG is entirely non-invasive and may be cheaper and faster than current techniques.

Ground-based and airborne high temperature SQUIDs have been used successfully in geophysical surveying trials. In Germany, high temperature SQUIDs are used to examine commercial aircraft wheels for possible flaws produced by the stress and heat generated at landing.

The advantage of the higher operating temperature of high temperature SQUIDs is exemplified in "SQUID microscopes," in which the device, mounted in vacuum just below a thin window, can be brought very close to samples at room temperature and pressure. Such microscopes are used to detect flaws in semiconductor chips and to monitor the gyrations of magnetotactic bacteria, which contain a tiny magnet for navigational purposes.

Although SQUIDs dominate the small-scale arena, other devices are important. Most national standards laboratories around the world use the ac Josephson effect to maintain the standard volt. Superconducting detectors are revolutionizing submillimeter and far infrared astronomy. Mixers involving a low temperature superconductor-insulator-superconductor (SIS) tunnel junction provide unrivaled sensitivity to narrowband signals, for example, those produced by rotational transitions of molecules in interstellar space. Roughly 100 SIS mixers are operational on ground-based radio telescopes, and a radio-telescope array planned for Chile will require about 1,000 such mixers. When one requires broadband detectors—for example, for the detection of the cosmic background radiation—the low temperature superconducting-transition-edge bolometer is the device of choice in the submillimeter range. The bolometer absorbs incident radiation, and the resulting rise in its temperature is detected by the change in resistance of a superconductor at its transition; this change is read out by a SQUID. Arrays of 1,000 or even 10,000 such bolometers are contemplated for satellite-based telescopes for rapid mapping of the cosmos—not only in the far infrared but also for X-ray astronomy. Superconducting detectors are poised to play a crucial role in radio and X-ray astronomy.

A rapidly growing number of cellular base stations use multipole high temperature filters on their receivers, yielding sharper bandwidth definition and lower noise than conventional filters. This technology enables the provider to pack more channels into a given frequency allocation in urban environments and to extend the distance between rural base stations.

The Next Millennium

The major fundamental questions are "Why are high temperature superconductors superconducting?" and "Can we achieve still higher temperature superconductors?" On the applications front, the development of a high temperature wire that can be manufactured cost effectively in sufficient lengths could revolutionize power generation, transmission, and utilization. On the small-scale end, superconducting detector arrays on satellites may yield new insights into the origins of our Universe. High temperature filters will provide rapid internet access from our cell phones. The combination of SQUID arrays and MRI will revolutionize our understanding of brain function. And perhaps a SQUID will even catch an axion.

Reprinted with permission from *Beam Line: A Periodical of Particle Physics*, Vol. 30, No. 2, 2000.

The development of nanolasers is a prime example of nanotechnological advancement in the 1990s. Nanolasers are made up of photon particles that are amplified by reflecting the beams between mirrors. Devices that emit these lasers exist at the nanometer scale, and at this minuscule size, the speed and efficiency of photon transmission are greatly improved when compared to their electronic counterparts. Thus, you can imagine an optical computer, in which the transmission of information is conducted through laser emission rather than electrical conduction. Although the concept of the optical computer is not quite a reality yet, nanolasers are already being used for a variety of other applications. For instance, one type of nanolaser—the biocavity laser—is being used to distinguish different types of cells during diagnosis of diseases such as cancer. The precision of the devices is useful for detecting subtle differences at the microscopic level. Automation of these nanolasers can improve the accuracy and efficiency of clinical diagnostic procedures.

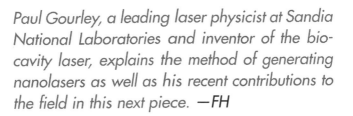

Paul Gourley, a leading laser physicist at Sandia National Laboratories and inventor of the bio-cavity laser, explains the method of generating nanolasers as well as his recent contributions to the field in this next piece. —FH

"Nanolasers"
by Paul L. Gourley
Scientific American, 1998

For decades, silicon transistors have become smaller and smaller, allowing the fabrication of tiny but powerful chips. Less well known is the parallel revolution of semi-conductor lasers. Recently researchers have shrunk some of the dimensions of such devices to an astonishing scale of nanometers (billionths of meters), even smaller than the wavelength of the light they produce. At such sizes—less than one hundredth the thickness of a human hair—curious aspects of quantum physics begin to take over. By exploiting this quantum behavior, researchers can tailor the basic characteristics of the devices to achieve even greater efficiencies and faster speeds.

Nanolasers could have myriad applications, for instance, in optical computers, where light would replace electricity for transporting, processing and storing information. Even though light-based computing may not occur anytime soon, other uses, such as in fiber-optic communications, have now become increasingly practical. With other researchers, I am also investigating the new lasers for novel purposes, such as the early detection of disease.

Jumping Electrons

Although nanolasers push the boundaries of modern physics, the devices work much like their earliest ancestor, a contraption fashioned from a rod of dark ruby more than 35 years ago. Essentially, a lasing material—for example, a gas such as helium or neon, or a crystalline semiconductor—is sandwiched between two mirrors. The substance is "pumped" with light or electricity. The process excites the electrons in the material to hop from lower to higher energy levels. When the electrons return to the lower stations, they produce light, which is reflected between the mirrors.

The bouncing photons trigger other "excited" electrons—those in higher energy states—to emit identical photons, much like firecrackers that pop and set off other firecrackers. This chain reaction is called stimulated emission. (Hence the name "laser," which is an acronym for "light amplification by stimulated emission of radiation.") As the number of photons grows, they become part of a communal wave that intensifies, finally bursting through one of the mirrors in a concentrated, focused beam.

But not all the photons take part in this wave. In fact, many are emitted spontaneously, apart from the chain reaction. In a large space—to a subatomic particle, the size of a typical laser cavity is immense—photons are relatively free to do what they want. Thus, many of the free-spirited photons are literally on a different wavelength, and they can scatter in all directions, often hitting the sides of the laser and generating unwanted heat instead of bouncing between the mirrors. For some types of lasers, only one photon in 10,000 is useful.

Because of this enormous waste, a certain threshold of energy is necessary to ensure that the number of excited electrons is large enough to induce and maintain stimulated emission. The requirement is analogous to the minimum amount of heat needed to bring a pot of water to boil. If the hurdle is not cleared, the laser will fail to attain the self-sustaining chain reaction crucial to its operation. This obstacle is why semiconductor lasers have required relatively high currents to work, in contrast to silicon transistors, which are much more frugal. But if semiconductor lasers could stop squandering energy, they could become competitive with their electronic counterparts for a host of applications, including their use in computers.

Recently the concept of "thresholdless" operation has become increasingly favored by many physicists. Proposed by Yoshihisa Yamamoto of NTT Basic Research Laboratories and Stanford University and Takeshi Kobayashi of Osaka University in Japan, thresholdless operation calls for all photons, even those spontaneously born, to be drafted into lasing duty. In theory, the device would require only the tiniest amount of energy, almost like a special kettle that could boil water with the heat of just a single match. Researchers disagree about the best design of such a laser. The consensus, though, is that the dimensions must be extraordinarily small—on the order of the wavelength of light emitted—so that the devices could take advantage of quantum behavior.

A New Generation

The groundwork for thresholdless operation was set in the late 1970s, when Kenichi Iga and other researchers at the Tokyo Institute of Technology demonstrated a radically different type of semiconductor laser [see "Microlasers," by J. L. Jewell, J. P. Harbison and A. Scherer; SCIENTIFIC AMERICAN, November 1991]. Popularly referred to as microlasers because of their micron-size dimensions, these devices are cousins to the semiconductor diode lasers widely found in compact-disc players. ("Diode" refers to a one-way flow of electricity during operation.)

Microlasers, however, differ from their common diode relatives in several fundamental ways. The latter are shaped like rectangular boxes that must be cleaved, or diced, from a large wafer, and they issue light longi-tudinally from the cut edges. Microlasers are smaller, cylindrical shapes formed by etching, and they emit light from the top—perpendicular to the round layers of semiconductor material that make up the device. Therefore, microlasers produce more perfectly circular beams. In addition, they can be built and tested many at a time in arrays on a wafer, similar to the way in which computer chips are fabricated. In contrast, diode lasers must generally be tested individually after having been diced into separate units.

Perhaps more important, microlasers exploit the quantum behavior of both electrons and photons. The devices are built with a "well"—an extremely thin layer of semiconductor only several atoms thick. In such a minute space, electrons can exist only at certain discrete, or quantized, energy levels separated by forbidden territory, called the band gap of the semiconductor. By sandwiching the quantum well with other material, researchers can trap electrons and force them to jump across the band gap to emit just the right kind of light.

Microlasers must also imprison photons to function. To accomplish this feat, engineers take advantage of the same effect that causes a transparent window to display a faint reflection. This phenomenon results from glass having a higher refractive index than air—that is, photons move more slowly through glass. When light passes between materials with different refractive indices, some of the photons are reflected at the border. The mirrors of microlasers consist of alternating layers of semiconductors with different refractive indices (such as gallium arsenide and aluminum arsenide). If the layers are just one quarter of a wavelength thick, the geometry of the structure will allow the weak reflections to reinforce one another. For the coupling of gallium arsenide and aluminum arsenide, a dozen pairs of layers will bounce back 99 percent of the light—a performance superior to that of polished metal mirrors commonly found in bathrooms.

Already the first crop of microlasers has found commercial applications in fiber-optic communications. Other uses are currently under investigation. Meanwhile ongoing work continues to refine the structures. In one recent device, certain layers are selectively oxidized, which helps to raise the population of excited electrons and bouncing photons in the well area, resulting in an operating efficiency greater than 50 percent. In other words, the laser is able to convert more than half the input energy into output laser light. This performance far exceeds that of semiconductor diode lasers, which are typically not even 30 percent efficient.

Microlasers have led to a new generation of devices that exploits electronic quantum behavior further. Scientists have now built structures such as quantum wires and dots that confine electrons to one and zero dimensions, respectively. (Wells restrict them to two.) Additionally, in a fundamentally new device called the quantum-cascade laser, researchers at Bell Laboratories have strung together many quantum wells, like a series of small waterfalls. In such a laser, an electron returning to a lower energy state will not take one big band-gap jump but multiple smaller ones, emitting a photon at each successive hop—thereby increasing the lasing chain reaction. An exciting feature of this innovative laser is that it allows engineers to tailor the type of light produced by adjusting the width of the wells; therefore, the electronic band gap of the material—a property ordained by nature—no longer dictates the kind of photons produced.

In a separate but related track of research, scientists have been exploring quantum-optical behavior. To do so, investigators have had to shrink some of the dimensions of the devices to smaller than even the wavelength of the light emitted. In that microscopic world, photons are restricted to certain discrete states, similar to the restraints placed on electrons trapped in quantum wells.

A Short Guitar String

Large lasers emit various types of photons, just as a long guitar string, when strummed, produces a sound consisting of a fundamental frequency (corresponding to the pitch) and many overtones. But as the guitar string is made shorter, the pitch becomes higher and the number of overtones decreases until the process reaches a limit decreed by the thickness and type of material of the string.

Similarly, physicists have been shrinking lasers to restrict the number of states, or modes, that the photons can inhabit. A limit to this miniaturization is one half the wavelength of the light emitted, because this dimension is the smallest for which the light is able to bounce between the mirrors. At this minimum boundary, photons would have just one possible state, corresponding to the fundamental optical mode of the device. Because of this Hobson's choice, every photon would be forced to contribute to the communal wave (the fundamental mode) that intensifies into the beam of light that finally bursts through one of the mirrors. In other words, no photons would go to waste: the laser would be thresholdless.

With colleagues at Sandia National Laboratories, I observed such quantized photon states in experiments more than a decade ago. By bringing the end mirrors of a microlaser closer, we were able to squeeze the broad spectrum of photons emitted into just a few optical modes. We showed that these modes occurred at wavelengths whose integral multiples were equal to the round-trip distance between the mirrors, in the same way that a guitar string can vibrate with four or five wavelengths between its fixed ends but not with four and one-sixth wavelengths. Furthermore, we verified that we could enhance these effects by moving the mirrors closer, approaching the limit of one half wavelength (hundreds of nanometers). But these devices were not yet thresholdless. Even the most advanced microlasers, which might now be legitimately called nanolasers, allow about 100 photonic states—much improved from the tens of thousands of options available to photons in conventional diode lasers but still not acceptable for entrance into thresholdless nirvana.

To achieve that ideal, researchers have recently begun to investigate other nanometer-scale geometries. One such design is the microdisk laser, developed by Richart E. Slusher and his colleagues at Bell Labs. With advanced etching processes similar to those used to fabricate computer chips, the Bell Labs researchers have been able to carve an ultrathin disk a couple of microns in diameter and just 100 nanometers thick. The semiconductor disk is surrounded by air and supported by a tiny pedestal, making the overall structure look like a microscopic table.

Because the semiconductor and air have very different indices of refraction, light generated inside the disk reflects within the structure, skimming along its circumference. The effect is similar to the "whispering gallery" sound waves first described by Lord Rayleigh more than a century ago. The physicist explained how conversations can be heard at opposite ends inside the great dome of St. Paul's Cathedral in London because the audible vibrations reflect off the walls and reinforce one another.

The tiny size of the microdisk restricts the photons to just a limited number of states, including the desired fundamental optical mode, while the whispering-gallery effect confines the photons until the light wave generated has built up enough energy to burst outside the structure. The result is extremely efficient operation with a low threshold. In fact, these microdisk lasers have worked with only about 100 microamps.

A variation of the microdisk is the microring laser, which is essentially a photonic wire curled into the shape of an ultraskinny doughnut. Seng-Tiong Ho and his colleagues at Northwestern University used microlithography to etch such a semiconductor structure with a diameter of 4.5 microns and a rectangular cross section measuring only 400 by 200 nanometers. To improve the quality of the light emitted, the Northwestern researchers surrounded the microring with a U-shaped glass structure that guides the photons out in two parallel beams along the legs of the U.

These novel devices have proved how the size and shape of a nanolaser can affect its operation by controlling the quantum behavior of the photons emitted. Investigators have recently pushed the technology even further, shrinking photonic wires to an amazing volume of just one fifth of a cubic micron. At that dimension, the structure has fewer than 10 photonic states—which approaches the conditions required for thresholdless operation.

Although these new nanolasers have reduced the *types* of photons to quantum-mechanical levels, they have not decreased the *number* of photons to such limits. With a small enough population, the behavior of light can be fundamentally altered for useful purposes. In recent landmark work, researchers at the Massachusetts Institute of Technology have shown that single excited atoms of barium can be fed one by one into a laser, with each atom emitting a useful photon. This incredibly efficient device is able to work with just 11 photons bouncing between the mirrors. Physicists are currently investigating such novel quantum optics for semiconductor nanolasers.

Stopping Light Periodically

A radically different approach to the design of nanolasers is to build a structure with materials that alternate at regular tiny intervals. If designed properly, the periodic modulation will imprison light by repeatedly reflecting it within the structure. This concept was first deployed by scientists who engineered the layered mirrors of microlasers, which contain light in one dimension. Eli Yablonovitch, now at the University of California at Los Angeles, and researchers at the Department of Energy Ames Laboratory at Iowa State University extended the principle into two and three dimensions by proposing new structures called photonic lattices.

The overall concept is based on a phenomenon observed in the early 1900s by the father-and-son team of William Henry Bragg and William Lawrence Bragg. The English physicists, who shared a Nobel Prize in

1915, studied how x-rays striking a crystal will backscatter in a manner dependent on the periodic structure of the crystal lattice. In what is now known as Bragg's law, the two scientists stated that the intensity of reflected radiation depends on three factors: the wavelength of the x-rays, the spacing of the atoms in the crystal and the angle at which the x-rays strike the lattice.

Applying this knowledge to optical frequencies, investigators such as Thomas F. Krauss and Richard M. De La Rue of the University of Glasgow have shown that a lattice of two different alternating materials will backscatter light in a similar way. Furthermore, by using materials of very different indices of refraction and by selecting the right periodic spacing between those substances, researchers have shown that they can tailor and extend the range of wavelengths that the device reflects, in effect creating a "photonic band gap" similar to the forbidden territory of electrons in semiconductors.

At Sandia, Joel Wendt, Allen Vawter and I fabricated such a structure by building a hexagonal lattice of gallium arsenide posts—a design that was developed by John D. Joannopoulos and other researchers at M.I.T. By taking into account the different indices of refraction of gallium arsenide and the surrounding air, we determined the exact spacing of the posts necessary to trap infrared light.

Although we have demonstrated the feasibility of confining light in this two-dimensional array, we have not yet been able to turn the structure into a laser. One possible way to do so would be to pump one of the posts, making it emit light, which would then be repeatedly reflected (and effectively contained) by the other posts in the array. Basically, the lattice would act like the parallel mirrors in a traditional laser.

Using a reverse design in which the "posts" are made of air and the surrounding material is a semiconductor, the M.I.T. researchers have fabricated a tiny silicon bridge (470 nanometers wide and 200 nanometers thick) etched lengthwise with a single row of microscopic holes. Light is confined to traveling across the structure because of the difference in indices of refraction between the semiconductor and the surrounding air.

The M.I.T. scientists, including Joannopoulos, Pierre R. Villeneuve and Shanhui Fan, used computer simulations to determine the precise periodic spacing of the holes in order to define a one-dimensional array suitable for confining infrared light. Furthermore, the researchers introduced a "defect" into the lattice by making the distance between two adjacent holes near the center of the strip slightly larger. The irregularity creates a fundamental optical mode within the minuscule volume circumscribed by the nonuniform spacing. This "box" might one day be developed into a laser cavity, with the adjacent holes acting like mirrors. Amazingly, the box is a mere twentieth of a cubic micron. The M.I.T. group has since refined the structure, building it on a glass base, and has verified the computer simulations with experimental results.

Other work has investigated photonic lattices that vary periodically in three dimensions. But such structures have been difficult to build because micro-fabrication techniques such as electron-beam lithography are more suited for the two-dimensional patterning of chipmaking. Still, three-dimensional photonic lattices would theoretically confine light in all directions—an ideal feature for a thresholdless laser.

Whither Optical Computers?

In addition to higher efficiency, thresholdless operation could lead to ultra-fast devices, which can be switched on and off instantaneously because they require such little energy for lasing to occur. In other words, waiting for a pot of water to boil can be brief if just one match will do the trick. Already some lasers can be switched on and off faster than 20 billion times a second.

Such blinding speeds are a natural for fiber-optic communications. Other applications will arise as these devices continue to become even faster, smaller and more energy-efficient. Thresholdless lasers, now a distinct possibility because of recent advances in the fabrication of structures of nanometer scale, hold great promise as components for transmitting, storing and manipulating information—that is, as the crucial building blocks for an optical computer. Ironically, advances in the shrinking of silicon transistors have enabled substantial improvements in semiconductor lasers, which could one day power computers and replace those tiny electronic circuits with optical ones.

5 The Future of Quantum Physics

The future possibilities for quantum physics in technology seem limitless. It is only a matter of time before quantum computers become household items, so quantum researchers are already thinking about the next advancement. Scientists hope to link quantum computers together through quantum networks. This would allow computers within a network to communicate with each other using quantum principles, thus enhancing the speed and capacity to exchange information. The concept of entanglement is central to the development of quantum networks, since this principle allows the instantaneous transfer of information from one place to another without traveling through space, otherwise known as quantum teleportation. Experimentally, scientists have succeeded in teleporting photons and other small particles. However, translating these successes into the transmission of information through quantum networks and even the futuristic quantum Internet still needs more

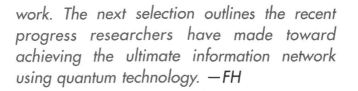

work. The next selection outlines the recent progress researchers have made toward achieving the ultimate information network using quantum technology. —FH

"Quantum Internet: Possible Use of Quantum Mechanics in Computer Networks"
by Peter Weiss
Science News, 1999

The quirks of quantum mechanics may lead to better computer networks.

Feverish experimentation now under way in labs around the world may one day lead to quantum computers. These extraordinarily powerful calculating machines would employ as their bits not electric circuits but particles that obey the strange rules of quantum mechanics. These devices are years away at best—maybe decades, maybe more.

Scientists dare to dream, anyway—not only of quantum computers but also of linking them together into networks. The connections between the machines would operate on quantum mechanical principles, too.

Fueling those dreams is a growing ability to transfer delicate quantum information from one place to another. New experiments that stretch quantum mechanical effects across distances of kilometers are providing encouragement.

Theorists are fanning the flames as well. Studies of how such hypothetical networks would compare with conventional ones hint that greater computing power waits to be unleashed.

H. Jeff Kimble, an experimenter and theorist at the California Institute of Technology in Pasadena, foresees such networks having a widespread impact. "One could imagine a quantum Internet in the future," he says. It would be a more complex web than the one that currently spans the globe and would employ communication capabilities not possible with conventional technology.

"Such a network can do heroic things," he predicts.

Less than 2 years ago, scientists succeeded for the first time in making information appear to leap instantaneously from one place to another without passing through the intervening space. In independent experiments, scientists in two European laboratories transferred a characteristic of one photon—the elementary particle of light—to another photon via a technique called quantum teleportation (SN: 1/17/98, p. 41). Researchers say quantum teleportation will be an essential ingredient of both quantum computers and networks.

Teleporting a photon's state is the equivalent of sending just one quantum bit, or qubit, worth of information. Unlike a conventional bit, which must represent either 0 or 1, a qubit represents a mixture of 0 and 1 called a superposition. Only when a measurement is actually made, which destroys the superposition, is the qubit forced into a specific value.

While wonderfully versatile, a qubit still packs only one nugget of information. Recently Kimble and

his colleagues have shown experimentally that quantum teleportation using light beams, made up of many photons, may be able to carry a great deal more information, enough perhaps to support practical computing.

Kimble's team and scientists from Aarhus University in Denmark and the University of Wales in Bangor shipped a characteristic of a pulse of light across a lab bench to another pulse a meter away. Although the distance is short, in principle the same technique could work over unlimited spans, Kimble says. The researchers described their experiment in the Oct. 23, 1998 SCIENCE.

"With our quantum scheme, we could take the whole output of a quantum computer and teleport it," says Christopher A. Fuchs, one of the Caltech researchers.

To achieve teleportation, scientists exploit another of the quantum realm's strange aspects. Known as entanglement, it creates a correlation between quantum objects that, in theory, persists no matter how far apart those entities become. The correlation arises because the objects occupy a joint quantum state. When the entanglement ends—because of a measurement, for example—the once-entangled states must adopt related values. Two formerly entangled photons would take on predictable characteristics—for instance, opposite values.

Kimble's team split a single laser beam to create an entangled pair of beams. One blazed into the sending station and the other into the receiving station. When a new pulse, which can be thought of as the message, interacts with the sending half of the original beam, entanglement requires that the receiving part be affected, too. In essence, the receiver gets a part of the message as quantum information via entanglement.

Teleportation also requires a classical transfer of information—in Kimble's experiment, along wires. By correctly combining the information from the wires and the beams, the scientists recreate the message at the receiving end.

Along the classical path, information flows no faster than the speed of light. So, quantum teleportation still obeys that universal speed limit.

Although light-based quantum-information pro-cessing seems promising, the quantum Internet may not ultimately use light as its medium. Attempts to use photons as bits in rudimentary quantum-computing experiments have run into some serious snags. In an alternative pursued by some researchers, the quantum Internet might slosh more than blink.

A number of scientific teams are exploring quan-tum computing and communication using atoms in liquids manipulated via nuclear magnetic resonance (NMR). The technique is also used in medicine to make images of body parts. With strong magnetic fields and radiowave pulses, NMR manipulates the spins of atomic nuclei.

In the Nov. 5, 1998 NATURE, researchers from Los Alamos (N.M.) National Laboratory and the University of New Mexico in Albuquerque reported a short-distance example of teleportation. They transmitted a characteris-tic known as spin orientation from one atom to another within a molecule. The scientists manipulated molecules of trichloroethylene dissolved in chloroform.

"We've used different nuclei to transfer the information, not photons or electromagnetic fields. We're the first ones to do that," says Raymond Laflamme of Los Alamos.

In a manner analogous to the optical experiments, the researchers created a quantum conduit by entangling two atoms. Then, they allowed another atom, which carried the spin message, to interact with one of the entangled pair, automatically affecting the other via the quantum link.

Although no wires were involved, a classical ingredient was still present. A combination of radiofrequency pulses and quiescent periods guided the molecule into a final state that depends on the arrangement of spins caused by the initial message interaction. Those influences finally nudged the target atom into the message's spin state.

The Caltech and Los Alamos achievements are both "great experimental tours de force in learning how to control these things," says Charles H. Bennett of the IBM Thomas J. Watson Research Center in Yorktown Heights, N.Y. Bennett is one of six theorists who in 1993 came up with the idea of quantum teleportation (SN: 4/10/93, p. 229).

Kimble, however, harbors grave doubts about the NMR experiment. "In my view, it's not a demonstration of teleportation, it's a simulation," he says. He contends that entanglements can't survive in the disorderly sea of molecules constituting a typical liquid. NMR proponents counter that Kimble and his fellow skeptics have chosen to ignore other analyses showing that entanglements can survive.

Teleporting across a molecule—or even a workbench—won't suffice for making practical networks. Researchers are building up to greater leaps, however, by testing the notion that entanglement has an unlimited range.

Wolfgang Tittel and his colleagues at the University of Geneva hold the world record for extending entanglement across space. Using existing optical fibers that had been installed for telecommunications, the scientific team split up entangled pairs of photons produced in Geneva and sent them on separate paths to Bellevue and Bernex, two villages outside Geneva (SN: 2/10/96, p. 90). The Swiss researchers used a different characteristic of photons than that transmitted in the teleportation experiments.

Measurements at the destinations determined that the quantum states remained correlated throughout the photons' journeys. In the May 1998 PHYSICAL REVIEW A, the researchers concluded, borrowing a phrase from Albert Einstein, that the "spooky action at a distance" between their entangled photons does not break down across the 10.9 kilometers between the villages.

Scientists are planning to test longer entanglements. Anton Zeilinger of the University of Vienna says that his group is gearing up for experiments at distances beyond 20 km. He led one of the first experiments in photon teleportation more than a year ago, while at the University of Innsbruck in Austria. His newly established Vienna lab will collaborate on the project with the Geneva researchers and other scientists.

To go beyond entanglement, the Vienna researchers are also laying plans for the first teleportation of a photon's characteristics across kilometer distances, Zeilinger says.

Those experiments would follow on an achievement completed while he was still at Innsbruck but just reported in the Feb. 15 PHYSICAL REVIEW LETTERS. The Innsbruck team simultaneously entangled three photons, with distances of roughly 20 centimeters between each of them.

It's not the first report of three-particle entanglement. Laflamme and his colleagues made that claim in a NMR experiment last year involving three atoms in a molecule (SN: 9/12/98, p. 165).

The Innsbruck experiment, however, goes far beyond interatomic distances, albeit without coming close to practical network dimensions. Moreover, "the same procedure we used for 3 photons can now be generalized" to possibly as many as 10 photons, Zeilinger says.

Would quantum networks be worth the work that it will take to develop the quantum links that they will need? Theorists are probing how model networks might perform and comparing them with conventional, or classical, computer networks.

Each node of a quantum network would be a quantum computer. Such machines would calculate and perform logical operations using delicate strings of entangled qubits, each in a superposition of many states. So far no more than three-qubit, rough-hewn calculating experiments have appeared in labs. Not until that qubit number grows to thirty or forty and a robust technology emerges will quantum computers begin to make their mark, scientists say.

At that point, teleportation would provide the thread to tie the computers together. How far those threads might stretch remains to be seen. Tittel thinks 50 km is possible with current optical fiber technology.

If quantum computers start talking to each other, what would come next? Computer scientists have begun to address that question, although on a very abstract level.

In one sort of problem that they ponder, several very busy people try to arrange to meet for lunch. They let their computers, which know their jam-packed schedules, interact with each other in order to find a time slot in which all three people are free.

For conventional computers, researchers had already proved years ago that for schedules with some number, n, of time slots, no fewer than n bits would have to be exchanged by the machines. Early last year, however, a trio of computer scientists examined how quantum computers would solve the problem and reported that the number of bits needed would be significantly below n.

"By using quantum bits, rather than classical bits, you can save on communication," says Richard Cleve of the University of Calgary in Alberta, a member of the research team. For this particular problem, however, he notes, the quantum treatment requires more exchanges among the computers than a classical solution does.

An analysis of a more esoteric problem by Ran Raz of the Weizmann Institute in Rehovot, Israel, concludes that a quantum interaction saves on both the number of bits exchanged and the number of exchanges. Raz is scheduled to present his work in May in Atlanta at the 31st Annual Association for Computing Machinery's Symposium on Theory of Computing.

Another example of a possible quantum-network edge emerged at a January workshop on algorithms in quantum information processing at DePaul University in Chicago.

Some computing researchers study ways in which computers can evaluate the validity of mathematical proofs. In the interactive method, two computers, named Arthur and Merlin after the legendary king and sorcerer, have a chat. Merlin, who is wise but not always honest, presents the proof to Arthur. Limited both in brains and time, Arthur queries Merlin in an attempt to verify the proof.

Daunted by the proof itself, Arthur asks Merlin to carry out related calculations instead. By checking for consistency among Merlin's answers, Arthur can discern if the proof is valid.

In the case of conventional computers, the number of rounds of question-and-answer grows as the mathematical statement or equation under consideration becomes more complicated.

At the DePaul conference, however, John Watrous of the University of Montreal reported that a quantum Arthur and Merlin duo could determine the validity of the proof, no matter how convoluted its mathematical expression, in only two rounds of questioning. Watrous says that the finding rests on a widely accepted assumption that there is a certain type of complexity in the mathematics.

Watrous's new evidence of latent quantum network power has impressed Bennett. "This is another major step along the way," he says. For more than two computers, Watrous says, he expects a quantum approach also to yield a bonus, but he hasn't yet analyzed that situation in detail.

If researchers ultimately find ways to make quantum information leap far enough and wide enough, a quantum leap for networks may not be far behind.

Weiss, Peter. "Quantum Internet: Possible Use of Quantum Mechanics in Computer Networks." © *Science News*.

Quantum physics has played a large role in science fiction by lending basic concepts of particle behavior that can be embellished and written into fantasy. The idea of teleportation is a perfect example of the quantum physics fantasy. By understanding particles and being able to break them down, it is imaginable that broken-down particles can be instantly transported to another location by rebuilding the particles. Entanglement is the key concept in quantum physics that allows teleportation schemes to become a reality. Albert Einstein, Boris Podolsky, and Nathan Rosen first introduced entanglement in 1935, and entanglement is

sometimes referred to as the EPR effect. They studied entangled pairs of particles whereby one particle's quantum properties are correlated with another particle's position or momentum. Therefore, movement of one particle to a particular position allows the prediction of the corresponding particle's position. This is the essence of teleportation that is described by physicist Anton Zeilinger in the following selection from the April 2000 issue of Scientific American. —FH

"Quantum Teleportation"
by Anton Zeilinger
Scientific American, 2000

The scene is a familiar one from science-fiction movies and TV: an intrepid band of explorers enters a special chamber; lights pulse, sound effects warble, and our heroes shimmer out of existence to reappear on the surface of a faraway planet. This is the dream of teleportation—the ability to travel from place to place without having to pass through the tedious intervening miles accompanied by a physical vehicle and airline-food rations. Although the teleportation of large objects or humans still remains a fantasy, quantum teleportation has become a laboratory reality for photons, the individual particles of light.

Quantum teleportation exploits some of the most basic (and peculiar) features of quantum mechanics, a branch of physics invented in the first quarter of the

20th century to explain processes that occur at the level of individual atoms. From the beginning, theorists realized that quantum physics led to a plethora of new phenomena, some of which defy common sense. Technological progress in the final quarter of the 20th century has enabled researchers to conduct many experiments that not only demonstrate fundamental, sometimes bizarre aspects of quantum mechanics but, as in the case of quantum teleportation, apply them to achieve previously inconceivable feats.

In science-fiction stories, teleportation often permits travel that is instantaneous, violating the speed limit set down by Albert Einstein, who concluded from his theory of relativity that nothing can travel faster than light [see "Faster Than Light?" by Raymond Y. Chiao, Paul G. Kwiat and Aephraim M. Steinberg; SCIENTIFIC AMERICAN, August 1993]. Teleportation is also less cumbersome than the more ordinary means of space travel. It is said that Gene Roddenberry, the creator of *Star Trek*, conceived of the "transporter beam" as a way to save the expense of simulating landings and takeoffs on strange planets.

The procedure for teleportation in science fiction varies from story to story but generally goes as follows: A device scans the original object to extract all the information needed to describe it. A transmitter sends the information to the receiving station, where it is used to obtain an exact replica of the original. In some cases, the material that made up the original is also transported to the receiving station, perhaps as "energy" of some kind; in other cases, the replica is made of atoms and molecules that were already present at the receiving station.

Quantum mechanics seems to make such a teleportation scheme impossible in principle. Heisenberg's uncertainty principle rules that one cannot know both the precise position of an object and its momentum at the same time. Thus, one cannot perform a perfect scan of the object to be teleported; the location or velocity of every atom and electron would be subject to errors. Heisenberg's uncertainty principle also applies to other pairs of quantities, making it impossible to measure the exact, total quantum state of any object with certainty. Yet such measurements would be necessary to obtain all the information needed to describe the original exactly. (In *Star Trek* the "Heisenberg Compensator" somehow miraculously overcomes that difficulty.)

A team of physicists overturned this conventional wisdom in 1993, when they discovered a way to use quantum mechanics itself for teleportation. The team—Charles H. Bennett of IBM; Gilles Brassard, Claude Crépeau and Richard Josza of the University of Montreal; Asher Peres of Technion-Israel Institute of Technology; and William K. Wootters of Williams College—found that a peculiar but fundamental feature of quantum mechanics, entanglement, can be used to circumvent the limitations imposed by Heisenberg's uncertainty principle without violating it.

Entanglement

It is the year 2100. A friend who likes to dabble in physics and party tricks has brought you a collection of pairs of dice. He lets you roll them once, one pair at a time. You handle the first pair gingerly, remembering the fiasco with the micro-black hole last Christmas. Finally, you roll the two dice and get double 3. You roll the next pair. Double 6. The next: double 1. They always match.

The dice in this fable are behaving as if they were quantum entangled particles. Each die on its own is random and fair, but its entangled partner somehow always gives the correct matching outcome. Such behavior has been demonstrated and intensively studied with real entangled particles. In typical experiments, pairs of atoms, ions or photons stand in for the dice, and properties such as polarization stand in for the different faces of a die.

Consider the case of two photons whose polarizations are entangled to be random but identical. Beams of light and even individual photons consist of oscillations of electromagnetic fields, and polarization refers to the alignment of the electric field oscillations. Suppose that Alice has one of the entangled photons and Bob has its partner. When Alice measures her photon to see if it is horizontally or vertically polarized, each outcome has a 50 percent chance. Bob's photon has the same probabilities, but the entanglement ensures that he will get exactly the same result as Alice. As soon as Alice gets the result "horizontal," say, she knows that Bob's photon will also be horizontally polarized. Before Alice's measurement the two photons do not have individual polarizations; the entangled state specifies only that a measurement will find that the two polarizations are equal.

An amazing aspect of this process is that it doesn't matter if Alice and Bob are far away from each other; the process works so long as their photons' entanglement has been preserved. Even if Alice is on Alpha Centauri and Bob on Earth, their results will agree when they compare them. In every case, it is as if Bob's photon is magically influenced by Alice's distant measurement, and vice versa.

You might wonder if we can explain the entanglement by imagining that each particle carries within it some recorded instructions. Perhaps when we entangle the two particles, we synchronize some hidden mechanism within them that determines what results they will give when they are measured. This would explain away the mysterious effect of Alice's measurement on Bob's particle. In the 1960s, however, Irish physicist John Bell proved a theorem that in certain situations any such "hidden variables" explanation of quantum entanglement would have to produce results different from those predicted by standard quantum mechanics. Experiments have confirmed the predictions of quantum mechanics to a very high accuracy.

Austrian physicist Erwin Schrödinger, one of the co-inventors of quantum mechanics, called entanglement "the essential feature" of quantum physics. Entanglement is often called the EPR effect and the particles EPR pairs, after Einstein, Boris Podolsky and Nathan Rosen, who in 1935 analyzed the effects of entanglement acting across large distances. Einstein talked of it as "spooky action at a distance." If one tried to explain the results in terms of signals traveling between the photons, the signals would have to travel faster than the speed of light. Naturally, many people have wondered if this effect could be used to transmit information faster than the speed of light.

Unfortunately, the quantum rules make that impossible. Each local measurement on a photon, considered in isolation, produces a completely random result and so can carry no information from the distant location. It tells you nothing more than what the distant measurement result probabilities would be, depending on what was measured there. Nevertheless, we can put entanglement to work in an ingenious way to achieve quantum teleportation.

Putting Entangled Photons to Work

Alice and Bob anticipate that they will want to teleport a photon in the future. In preparation, they share an entangled auxiliary pair of photons, Alice taking photon A and Bob photon B. Instead of measuring them, they each store their photon without disturbing the delicate entangled state.

In due course, Alice has a third photon—call it photon X—that she wants to teleport to Bob. She does not know what photon X's state is, but she wants Bob to have a photon with that same polarization. She cannot simply measure the photon's polarization and send Bob the result. In general, her measurement result would not be identical to the photon's original state. This is Heisenberg's uncertainty principle at work.

Instead, to teleport photon X, Alice measures it jointly with photon A, without determining their individual polarizations. She might find, for instance, that their polarizations are "perpendicular" to each other (she still does not know the absolute polarization of either one, however). Technically, the joint measurement of photon A and photon X is called a Bell-state measurement. Alice's measurement produces a subtle effect: it changes Bob's photon to correlate with a combination of her measurement result and the state that photon X originally had. In fact, Bob's photon now carries her photon X's state, either exactly or modified in a simple way.

To complete the teleportation, Alice must send a message to Bob—one that travels by conventional means, such as a telephone call or a note on a scrap of paper. After he receives this message, if necessary Bob can transform his photon B, with the end result that it becomes an exact replica of the original photon X. Which transformation Bob must apply depends on the outcome of Alice's measurement. There are four possibilities, corresponding to four quantum relations between her photons A and X. A typical transformation that Bob must apply to his photon is to alter its polarization by 90 degrees, which he can do by sending it through a crystal with the appropriate optical properties.

Which of the four possible results Alice obtains is completely random and independent of photon X's original state. Bob therefore does not know how to process his photon until he learns the result of Alice's measurement. One can say that Bob's photon instantaneously contains all the information from Alice's original, transported there by quantum mechanics. Yet to know how to read that information, Bob must wait for the classical information, consisting of two bits that can travel no faster than the speed of light.

Skeptics might complain that the only thing teleported is the photon's polarization state or, more generally, its quantum state, not the photon "itself." But because a photon's quantum state is its defining characteristic, teleporting its state is completely equivalent to teleporting the particle.

Note that quantum teleportation does not result in two copies of photon X. Classical information can be copied any number of times, but perfect copying of quantum information is impossible, a result known as the no-cloning theorem, which was proved by Wootters and Wojciech H. Zurek of Los Alamos National Laboratory in 1982. (If we could clone a quantum state, we could use the clones to violate Heisenberg's principle.) Alice's measurement actually entangles her photon A with photon X, and photon X loses all memory, one might say, of its original state. As a member of an entangled pair, it has no individual polarization state. Thus, the original state of photon X disappears from Alice's domain.

Circumventing Heisenberg

Furthermore, photon X's state has been transferred to Bob with neither Alice nor Bob learning anything about what the state is. Alice's measurement result, being entirely random, tells them nothing about the state. This is how the process circumvents Heisenberg's principle, which stops us from determining the complete quantum state of a particle but does not preclude teleporting the complete state so long as we do not try to see what the state is!

Also, the teleported quantum information does not travel materially from Alice to Bob. All that travels materially is the message about Alice's measurement result, which tells Bob how to process his photon but carries no information about photon X's state itself.

In one out of four cases, Alice is lucky with her measurement, and Bob's photon immediately becomes an identical replica of Alice's original. It might seem as if information has traveled instantly from Alice to Bob, beating Einstein's speed limit. Yet this strange feature cannot be used to send information, because Bob has no way of knowing that his photon is already an identical replica. Only when he learns the result of Alice's Bell-state measurement, transmitted to him via classical means, can he exploit the information in the teleported quantum state. Suppose he tries to guess in which cases teleportation was instantly successful. He will be wrong 75 percent of the time, and he will not know which guesses were correct. If he uses the photons based on such guesses, the results will be the same as if he had taken a beam of photons with random polarizations. In this way, Einstein's relativity prevails; even the spooky instantaneous action at a distance of quantum mechanics fails to send usable information faster than the speed of light.

It would seem that the theoretical proposal described above laid out a clear blueprint for building a teleporter; on the contrary, it presented a great experimental challenge. Producing entangled pairs of photons has become routine in physics experiments in the past decade, but carrying out a Bell-state measurement on two independent photons had never been done before.

Building a Teleporter

A powerful way to produce entangled pairs of photons is spontaneous parametric down-conversion: a single photon passing through a special crystal sometimes generates two new photons that are entangled so that they will show opposite polarization when measured.

A much more difficult problem is to entangle two independent photons that already exist, as must occur during the operation of a Bell-state analyzer. This means that the two photons (A and X) somehow have to lose their private features. In 1997 my group (Dik Bouwmeester, Jian-Wei Pan, Klaus Mattle, Manfred Eibl and Harald Weinfurter), then at the University of Innsbruck, applied a solution to this problem in our teleportation experiment.

In our experiment, a brief pulse of ultraviolet light from a laser passes through a crystal and creates the entangled photons A and B. One travels to Alice, and the other goes to Bob. A mirror reflects the ultraviolet pulse back through the crystal again, where it may create another pair of photons, C and D. (These will also be entangled, but we don't use their entanglement.) Photon C goes to a detector, which alerts us that its partner D is available to be teleported. Photon D passes through a polarizer, which we can orient in any conceivable way. The resulting polarized photon is our photon X, the one to be teleported, and travels on to Alice. Once it passes through the polarizer, X is an independent photon, no longer entangled. And although we know its polarization because of how we set the polarizer, Alice does not. We reuse the same ultraviolet pulse in this way to ensure that Alice has photons A and X at the same time.

Now we arrive at the problem of performing the Bell-state measurement. To do this, Alice combines her two photons (A and X) using a semireflecting mirror, a device that reflects half of the incident light. An individual photon has a 50-50 chance of passing through or being reflected. In quantum terms, the photon goes into a superposition of these two possibilities.

Now suppose that two photons strike the mirror from opposite sides, with their paths aligned so that the reflected path of one photon lies along the transmitted path of the other, and vice versa. A detector waits at the end of each path. Ordinarily the two photons would be reflected independently, and there would be a 50 percent chance of them arriving in separate detectors. If the photons are indistinguishable and arrive at the mirror at the same instant, however, quantum interference takes place: some possibilities cancel out and do not occur, whereas others reinforce and occur more often. When the photons interfere, they have only a 25 percent likelihood of ending up in separate detectors. Furthermore, when that occurs it corresponds to detecting one of the four possible Bell states of the two photons—the case that we called "lucky" earlier. The other 75 percent of the time the two photons both end up in one detector, which corresponds to the other three Bell states but does not discriminate among them.

When Alice simultaneously detects one photon in each detector, Bob's photon instantly becomes a replica of Alice's original photon X. We verified that this teleportation occurred by showing that Bob's photon had the polarization that we imposed on photon X. Our experiment was not perfect, but the correct polarization was detected 80 percent of the time (random photons would achieve 50 percent). We demonstrated the procedure with a variety of polarizations: vertical, horizontal, linear at 45 degrees and even a nonlinear kind of polarization called circular polarization.

The most difficult aspect of our Bell-state analyzer is making photons A and X indistinguishable. Even the timing of when the photons arrive could be used to identify which photon is which, so it is important to "erase" the time information carried by the particles. In our experiment, we used a clever trick first suggested by Marek Zukowski of the University of Gdansk: we send the photons through very narrow bandwidth wavelength filters. This process makes the wavelength of the photons very precise, and by Heisenberg's uncertainty relation it smears out the photons in time.

A mind-boggling case arises when the teleported photon was itself entangled with another and thus did not have its own individual polarization. In 1998 my Innsbruck group demonstrated this scenario by giving Alice photon D without polarizing it, so that it was still entangled with photon C. We showed that when the teleportation succeeded, Bob's photon B ended up entangled with C. Thus, the *entanglement* with C had been transmitted from A to B.

Piggyback States

Our experiment clearly demonstrated teleportation, but it had a low rate of success. Because we could identify just one Bell state, we could teleport Alice's photon only 25 percent of the time—the occasions when that state occurred. No complete Bell-state analyzer exists for independent photons or for any two independently created quantum particles, so at present there is no experimentally proven way to improve our scheme's efficiency to 100 percent.

In 1994 a way to circumvent this problem was proposed by Sandu Popescu, then at the University of Cambridge. He suggested that the state to be teleported could be a quantum state riding piggyback on Alice's auxiliary photon A. Francesco De Martini's group at the University of Rome I "La Sapienza" successfully demonstrated this scheme in 1997. The auxiliary pair of photons was entangled according to the photons' locations: photon A was split, as by a beam splitter, and sent to two different parts of Alice's apparatus, with the two alternatives linked by entanglement to a similar splitting of Bob's photon B. The state to be teleported was also carried by Alice's photon A—its polarization state. With both roles played by one photon, detecting all four possible Bell states becomes a standard single-particle measurement: detect Alice's photon in one of two possible locations with one of two possible polarizations. The drawback of the scheme is that if Alice were given a separate unknown state X to be teleported she would somehow have to transfer the state onto the polarization of her photon A, which no one knows how to do in practice.

Polarization of a photon, the feature employed by the Innsbruck and the Rome experiments, is a discrete quantity, in that any polarization state can be expressed as a superposition of just two discrete states, such as vertical and horizontal polarization. The electromagnetic field associated with light also has continuous features that amount to superpositions of an infinite number of basic states. For example, a light beam can be "squeezed," meaning that one of its properties is made extremely precise or noise-free, at the expense of greater randomness in another property (à la Heisenberg). In 1998 Jeffrey Kimble's group at the California Institute of Technology teleported such a squeezed state from one beam of light to another, thus demonstrating teleportation of a continuous feature.

Remarkable as all these experiments are, they are a far cry from quantum teleportation of large objects. There are two essential problems: First, one needs an entangled pair of the same kind of objects. Second, the object to be teleported and the entangled pairs must be sufficiently isolated from the environment. If any information leaks to or from the environment through stray interactions, the objects' quantum states degrade, a process called decoherence. It is hard to imagine how we could achieve such extreme isolation for a large piece of equipment, let alone a living creature that breathes air and radiates heat. But who knows how fast development might go in the future?

Certainly we could use existing technology to teleport elementary states, like those of the photons in our experiment, across distances of a few kilometers and maybe even up to satellites. The technology to teleport states of individual atoms is at hand today: the group led by Serge Haroche at the École Normale Supérieure in Paris has demonstrated entanglement of atoms. The entanglement of molecules and then their teleportation may reasonably be expected within the next decade. What happens beyond that is anybody's guess.

A more important application of teleportation might very well be in the field of quantum computation, where the ordinary notion of bits (0's and 1's) is generalized to quantum bits, or qubits, which can exist as superpositions and entanglements of 0's and 1's. Teleportation could be used to transfer quantum information between quantum processors. Quantum teleporters can also serve as basic components used to build a quantum computer.

Quantum mechanics is probably one of the profoundest theories ever discovered. The problems that it poses for our everyday intuition about the world led Einstein to criticize quantum mechanics very strongly. He insisted that physics should be an attempt to grasp a reality that exists independently of its observation.

Yet he realized that we run into deep problems when we try to assign such an independent physical reality to the individual members of an entangled pair. His great counterpart, Danish physicist Niels Bohr, insisted that one has to take into account the whole system—in the case of an entangled pair, the arrangement of both particles together. Einstein's desideratum, the independent real state of each particle, is devoid of meaning for an entangled quantum system.

Quantum teleportation is a direct descendant of the scenarios debated by Einstein and Bohr. When we analyze the experiment, we would run into all kinds of problems if we asked ourselves what the properties of the individual particles *really* are when they are entangled. We have to analyze carefully what it means to "have" a polarization. We cannot escape the conclusion that all we can talk about are certain experimental results obtained by measurements. In our polarization measurement, a click of the detector lets us construct a picture in our mind in which the photon actually "had" a certain polarization at the time of measurement. Yet we must always remember that this is just a made up story. It is valid only if we talk about that specific experiment, and we should be cautious in using it in other situations.

Indeed, following Bohr, I would argue that we can understand quantum mechanics if we realize that science is not describing how nature *is* but rather expresses what we can *say* about nature. This is where the current value of fundamental experiments such as teleportation lies: in helping us to reach a deeper understanding of our mysterious quantum world.

A pivotal point in quantum physics was the discovery of entanglement in 1935. Quantum entanglement refers to the phenomenon that the physical properties of interacting or entangled particles are related to each other, despite any distance that separates them. So when two particles bump into each other, the spin and momentum of each particle depends on the other. Entanglement is a critical principle in quantum physics and is the basis of several quantum actions such as teleportation and encryption. Although this phenomenon was originally thought to hold true only for minuscule particles such as photons, researchers are now applying the idea to larger-scale entities such as salts, superconductors, and time. The increased awareness of quantum physical processes such as entanglement will have profound effects on the future of technology, biology, and astronomy. Entanglement is applicable to multiple systems and transcends the boundaries within science, making it a revolutionary paradigm within quantum physics. The following article by

science writer Michael Brooks reviews the importance of entanglement and its intriguing presence in our world. —FH

"The Weirdest Link"
by Michael Brooks
New Scientist, **2004**

ENTANGLEMENT. Erwin Schrödinger called this phenomenon the defining trait of quantum theory. Einstein famously dubbed it *spukhafte Fernwirkungen*: "spooky action at a distance." It is not hard to understand why. Set things up correctly, and you can instantaneously affect the physical properties of a particle on the other side of the universe simply by prodding its entangled twin.

This is no longer just a curiosity of the quantum world, visible only in excruciatingly delicate experiments. Physicists now believe that entanglement between particles exists everywhere, all the time, and have recently found shocking evidence that it affects the wider, "macroscopic" world that we inhabit.

It is a discovery that might have far-reaching consequences. Not only will it give us a better grip on technological applications, such as quantum computing and cryptography, and the teleportation of quantum states, it could also open up a whole new realm of reality, enabling us to retain and control quantum weirdness in our everyday world. And it's not just a strange kind of "remote control" over matter that is at stake. Entanglement could even be

the key to understanding what gives rise to the phenomenon of life. It's enough to set Einstein spinning in his grave.

Entanglement has been an affront to our sensibilities for several decades now. Schrödinger discovered it through his newly formed quantum theory, when he examined the mathematical descriptions of two quantum particles that bump into one other. After the interaction, it is impossible to tease apart the two particles' characteristics. Once they are entangled, it makes no sense to talk about the properties of just one of them. All the information about the particles, such as their momentum and spin, lies only in their joint properties. So if something affects the quantum state of one particle, it will inevitably affect the quantum state of the other, no matter how far apart they are. It is this that gives entanglement the "spooky" character that Einstein found so distasteful.

Although it seems like something from the realm of fantasy, many physicists now use entanglement as a kind of resource for experiments and applications. Entangled pairs of quantum particles such as photons are routinely created and sent down microscopes or fired across vast distances. Their spooky properties are used to perform such feats as high-resolution imaging, quantum teleportation or quantum cryptography.

But, despite the growing use of entanglement as a technological tool, physicists are beginning to realise we have only just scratched the surface of its potential. "Are there some other forms of entanglement that we haven't yet discovered?" asks Benni Reznik, a theoretical physicist at Tel Aviv University in Israel. "I think there are."

Just how little we know about entanglement was made crystal clear last year by a collaboration led by Sayantani Ghosh at the University of Chicago (*Nature*, vol. 425, p. 48). The team analysed experiments done more than a decade ago with a sample of a magnetic salt containing holmium atoms, and compared them with theoretical predictions. What they found is extraordinary.

The holmium atoms within the salt behave like tiny magnets and respond to each others' magnetic fields by adjusting their relative orientation, just as a compass needle orients itself to align with the Earth's magnetic field. But the atoms change this settled orientation if they are placed in an external magnetic field. The degree to which they align with the field is known as the salt's "magnetic susceptibility."

Ghosh and his colleagues examined how the susceptibility of the salt varied with temperature. They expected it would decrease as the temperature rose, because the extra energy at higher temperatures disrupts the atoms' ability to maintain the optimum alignment. And it did. But at very low temperatures, the atoms were aligned to a greater degree than would be expected if they had normal quantum energy levels. The team believe that quantum entanglement between the atoms is the only explanation for this phenomenon.

It's a big shock: it shows that the quantum phenomenon of entanglement, whose power was thought to be confined to the infinitesimal world of subatomic

particles, can produce effects that remain measurable on macroscopic scales.

Ghosh and his colleagues also showed that entanglement affects the salt's heat capacity, defined as the amount of heat needed to change the temperature of a kilogram of substance by 1 kelvin. Throw in some heat, and you can only determine exactly how far the salt's temperature will rise if you take entanglement between atoms into account.

According to Vlatko Vedral, a theoretical physicist at Imperial College in London, these discoveries are highly important. Vedral was one of the team that first predicted the effect, three years ago (*Physical Review Letters*, vol. 87, p. 017901). The fact that the prediction has been borne out by experiment catapults the mystery of entanglement into the list of big unanswered questions that scientists need to address, he says.

That's partly because physicists can no longer content themselves with using the quantum and classical energy level descriptions of a material if they want to determine and understand its properties. The effects of entanglement now have to be included as an integral part of any accurate calculation.

But the results also suggest that, if we knew where to look, we might find entanglement causing significant effects in other materials. "It's not just magnetic salts—this should be a more universal thing," Vedral says.

The best place to look first, he believes, might be the enigmatic phenomenon of high-temperature superconductivity. Vedral points out that superconductors contain pairs of electrons whose quantum descriptions, or wave functions, appear to be entangled. "The wave function describing the pair is not equal to the product of two wave functions," he says. "Mathematically, I can see there is entanglement."

So should entanglement be considered as a possible cause of high-temperature superconductivity? Might it show us how to make materials that are superconducting at room temperature? At this stage, it is too early to say: the effects of entanglement on Ghosh's magnetic salt only become noticeable below 1 kelvin. "That is almost absolute zero," Vedral admits. "What would be really interesting would be to find a material that exhibits the effects of entanglement at higher temperatures." Eventually, he thinks, we might well find such a material at room temperature. "I don't think it's going to be a very easy search, but I can't think of anything that would rule this out on the basis of fundamental theory. It doesn't look impossible to me."

While this might seem hopelessly optimistic at first glance, other recent discoveries about entanglement are suggesting otherwise. Entanglements at room temperature appear to be an everyday part of the universe. Reznik, for instance, has shown that all of empty space—what physicists refer to as the vacuum—is filled with pairs of particles that are entangled. "It's an unusual idea," says Reznik. "It was quite hard to get our first paper on this accepted." His paper was finally published last year in *Foundations of Physics* (vol. 33, p. 167).

Thomas Durt of Vrije University in Brussels also believes entanglement is everywhere. He has recently shown, from the basic equations that Schrödinger considered, that almost all quantum interactions produce entanglement, whatever the conditions. "When you see light coming from a faraway star, the photon is almost certainly entangled with the atoms of the star and the atoms encountered along the way," he says. And the constant interactions between electrons in the atoms that make up your body are no exception. According to Durt, we are a mass of entanglements.

Curiouser and Curiouser

Of course, that is no guarantee we can use them. Reznik says he doesn't think you can take his vacuum entanglement and use it to perform feats such as teleportation. Indeed, he is not even sure how to demonstrate that this entanglement exists. Though the equations of quantum field theory show that it is present, he is still working out how to perform an experiment that makes vacuum entanglement more than a theoretical result.

These are all tantalising revelations, because they suggest that something priceless is within our grasp. But how do we reach it?

We certainly need to find a better handle on practical entanglement: at the moment, the only forms of it we have learned to use are somewhat constraining. The entangled photons used for cryptography and teleportation are produced by firing a photon into a "non-linear" crystal, such as beta barium borate. The optical properties of a non-linear crystal depend on its orientation, and a photon fired in at the correct angle will split into two entangled photons. But the entanglement between the photon pair is an artifact of the internal properties of the original photon—its path and polarisation (*New Scientist*, 30 October, 1999, p. 32). So entangled photons from a non-linear crystal effectively remain just one quantum system, rather than being the result of two distinct particles meeting and interacting. "It's a kind of entanglement, but not quite the same as between different quantum systems," Vedral says.

What physicists would dearly like, the resource that would open the way for the best experiments, is an unlimited source of pure two-particle entanglements. Despite the recent progress, this rich source of quantum magic has eluded them so far. So how do we take things forward? Schrödinger first discovered entanglement through analysing the mathematical descriptions of quantum theory, so perhaps mathematicians should be the pioneers. The trouble with this is that entanglement gives mathematicians a severe headache—especially when the entanglement is between anything more than two particles.

In theory, just bouncing particles off an entangled pair will establish another entanglement link that can then be put to work, but it's much easier said than done. Experimental physicists John Rarity and Paul Tapster were the first to entangle three photons, in their laboratory at the UK Defence Evaluation and Research Agency in Malvern, Worcestershire, five years ago. But no one has ever managed to work out how to describe the properties of such a system. For the most part, theorists can't even look at a given quantum state and tell if it is entangled—it is only possible in a few special cases. "Although I can define what it means to be entangled, that is, I can write down a state that's entangled and a state that's not, if you give me a state and ask whether it's entangled, then I have no efficient way of telling you that," says Vedral. In other words, he knows how to formulate the calculation, but it is so difficult that no computer can actually perform it.

But these problems may be nothing compared to the bombshell that Caslav Brukner of the University of Vienna has just dropped. As if our current understanding of entanglement between widely separated particles were not sketchy enough, Brukner, working with Vedral and two other Imperial College researchers, has uncovered a radical twist. They have shown that moments of time can become entangled too (www.arxiv.org/abs/quant-ph/0402127).

They achieved this through a thought experiment that examines how quantum theory links successive measurements of a single quantum system. Measure a photon's polarisation, for example, and you will get a particular result. Do it again some time later, and you will get a second result. What Brukner and Vedral have found is a strange connection between the past and the future: the very act of measuring the photon polarisation a second time can affect how it was polarised earlier on. "It's really surprising," says Vedral.

This entanglement between moments in time is so bizarre that it could expose a hole in the very fabric of quantum theory, the researchers believe. The formulation does not allow messages to be sent back in time, but it still means that quantum mechanics seems to be bending the laws of cause and effect. On top of that, entanglement in time puts space and time on an equal footing in quantum theory, and that goes sharply against the grain.

Space and time have always been very different in quantum theory. A location in space is an "observable"—like momentum or spin, spatial coordinates are just another property any quantum particle can have. The passing of time, on the other hand, has always been part of the backdrop. An electron can have a particular value of spin, or momentum or location, but it cannot have a particular time.

But if time can become entangled, it should be considered as an observable, and there is no way to write that into quantum theory. "People have tried, but something in quantum mechanics always has to be violated if you want a proper time-observable," Vedral says. "So it could be that something in quantum mechanics has to be reformulated."

In other words, Brukner's result suggests that we might be missing something important in our understanding of how the world works. Maybe that shouldn't surprise us. After all, entanglement between two spatially separated objects already tells us that space doesn't really have the form that classical physics says it does: instantaneous cause and effect across cosmological distances is not something that any theory of the universe can cope with. And now

Brukner's result seems to extend this "impossibility" to events separated in time as well.

It's not cause for despair, though. We know that relativity and quantum theory have to be meshed together if we are to create a "final" theory of how the universe works. It is too early to read much into Brukner's result, but maybe it is a clue about how to produce such a theory.

In the meantime, Vedral thinks he's identified an equally significant project to pursue. If, as Ghosh's result suggests, entanglement can produce macroscopic effects, is it such a stretch to reason that quantum entanglement might be the key to understanding life?

We know that quantum mechanics describes how atoms combine into molecules, and so underpins chemistry. And chemical processes underpin all biological processes, including the metabolic cycle and replication. So could entanglement support the emergent, macroscopic characteristic of chemistry that we call life? Reznik and Durt's revelations—that entanglements exist around us and inside us all the time—can only add to the intrigue. "I think it's a speculation worth making," Vedral says. "There may be some experiments in biology or biochemistry where we can see more of these effects, interpret some of the results in a different light. It would be a very exciting find."

Couple that with the ability to create materials that exploit our unfolding understanding of entanglement, and we might one day even gain the ability to use entanglement to create new forms of life. Now that is a spooky thought.

Reprinted with permission of *New Scientist.*

Traveling through time has long been an imaginary concept, deemed impossible by classical scientific thought. However, quantum physics has enabled scientists to approach time travel in new ways that, at least theoretically, make time travel possible. To understand these approaches, space has to be considered in four dimensions, rather than the conventional three. The fourth dimension is that of time, and together, these dimensions form space-time, which is a term used to describe an event that occurs at a specific place and time. A person's life consists of a series of events that occur in chronological order known as a world-line. It is possible to travel backward or forward in a particular space-time by considering closed timelike curves (CTCs), whereby a world-line is closed. This allows a person's life events to loop around and make shortcuts in time, otherwise known as wormholes. Physicist Michio Kaku helps us understand the possibilities of traveling through time through the use of these quantum physics concepts along with high-velocity travel

(faster than the speed of light) in the following selection published in Wired *magazine.* —FH

"A User's Guide to Time Travel"
by Michio Kaku
Wired, **2003**

Did the tech bubble burst in your face? Were you one of those unlucky outsiders who missed the Yahoo! IPO or got stuck with Enron stock long after the execs had dumped theirs? Wouldn't you like to be, just once, in the right place at the right time? Now you can. Follow a few simple instructions to relive the bull market and bail out just in time—then go on to march with Pericles or meet your great-great-great-grandchild.

Once confined to fantasy and science fiction, time travel is now simply an engineering problem. Physicists schooled in Newton's laws believed that time moved along a straight, steady course, like a speeding arrow. Then came Einstein in the early 1900s. His equations showed that time is more like a river. The more mass or energy you possess, the more the current around you varies. By moving at high velocity, for instance, you can make time slow down, and when you come to a stop, you'll be younger than if you'd remained at rest. Thus, a speedy spacecraft makes a fairly basic time machine.

Even after Einstein, most physicists believed the clock ticked in only one direction. While moving faster than the speed of light could, according to Einstein's equations, reverse time's arrow, such motion was impossible, because any object that reached that velocity would become infinite in mass. Trips to the past were preposterous.

Not anymore. Having examined Einstein's equations more closely, physicists now realize that the river of time may be diverted into a whirlpool—called a closed timelike curve—or even a fork leading to a parallel universe. In particular, the more mass you can concentrate at a single point, the more you can bend the flow.

In recent years, new designs for time machines have been flying off drawing boards at the world's top science labs. Exact specifications depend on where in time and space you wish to travel. You'll need a hefty CPU to solve the relevant equations for your machine's precise size, shape, motion, location, surroundings, and so on; the more accurately you can nail down these variables, the closer you'll come to your intended destination.

The designs that follow don't have the panache of Doc Brown's DeLorean in *Back to the Future* or even H. G. Wells' brass and quartz dream machine, but they do put time travel within reach of anyone with a couple of fast spaceships, a supercomputer, and a solar-system-scale machine shop. Warning: Time-space distortions may not be stable and may collapse as you enter, so approach them at your own risk. Also, when going back in time, do not—repeat—do not kill your parents before you are born. *Wired* takes no responsibility for parallel universes in which you find yourself trapped for eternity.

Thorne Plates

When Carl Sagan was writing his 1985 novel *Contact*, he asked Caltech physicist Kip Thorne how to abbreviate the lengthy flight time required for a trip to a distant star. Thorne suggested a wormhole, a shortcut through space-time that almost certainly exists as a consequence of Einsteinian principles, although one has yet to be detected. A few years later, Thorne suggested that a wormhole's entrances could be positioned in space and time as desired. Unlike some other time machines, this Thorne-inspired design allows round trips. However, it can't take you back to a time before the machine was built. Here's how it works:

- Obtain four large conductive plates at least a few miles in diameter. Arrange them in parallel, very close together. The space between each plate will teem with negative energy—a proven phenomenon known as the Casimir effect—creating slices of identical space-time.

- Separate the plates into two pairs. A wormhole will connect the pairs like an umbilical cord.

- Place one pair in a rocket ship and accelerate to almost the speed of light, preferably in a circular path so the rocket doesn't stray too far. Time will nearly freeze for that set while the other, still on the ground, ages at the usual rate. With each passing moment, the space-borne plates will go farther back in time relative to the others.

- When a sufficient amount of time has passed—preferably decades—step between the earthbound plates. You'll immediately be transported back in time and across space to the other pair.

Fine print: To activate Thorne plates, the distance between each plate must be less than the width of an atom. The resulting wormhole will be equally small, so getting in and out might be difficult. To widen the portal, some scientists suggest using a laser to inject immense amounts of negative energy. In addition, Thorne believes that radiation effects created by gravitons, or particles of gravity, might fry you as you enter the wormhole. According to string theory, however, this probably won't happen, so it's scant reason to cancel your trip.

Gott Loop

Many scientists believe the big bang that created the universe left behind cosmic strings—thin, infinitely long filaments of compressed matter. In 1991, Princeton physicist J. Richard Gott discovered that two of these structures, arranged in parallel and moving in opposite directions, would warp space-time to allow travel to the past. He later reworked the idea to involve a single cosmic-string loop. A Gott loop can take you back in time but not forward. The guide to building your own:

- Scan the galaxy for a loop of cosmic string.
- When you find one, fly close to it in a massive spaceship. Use the ship's gravity to shape the string into a rectangle roughly 54,000 light-years long and .01 light-years

wide. Gravity exerted by the longer sides of the rectangle will cause it to collapse, bringing the sides closer and closer together at nearly the speed of light.

- As the two sides approach within 10 feet of each other, circle them in a smaller ship. When you return to the start of the circle, you will have traveled back in time.

Fine print: To take you back one year, the string must weigh about half as much as the Milky Way galaxy. You'll need a mighty big spaceship to make that rectangle.

Gott Shell

In essence, a Gott shell is a huge concentration of mass. The shell's sheer density creates a gravitational field that slows down the clock for anyone enclosed within it. Outside, time rolls along at its familiar pace, but inside, it creeps. Thus the Gott shell is useful for travel into the future only. If you're planning a jaunt to the past using a Gott loop, you might want to bring along a Gott shell for the return trip. What to do, step by step:

- Salvage scrap planetary matter to assemble a mass equal to or greater than Jupiter's.

- Working slowly so as not to produce sudden gravitational disturbances, assemble the matter around yourself in a sphere. For your comfort—and to avoid inadvertently creating a black hole later in the process—be sure to leave a cavity larger than 18 feet in diameter at the center.

- Stock the cockpit with lots of food, drink, diversions, and back issues of *Wired*. Your journey might take a while.

- Using a high-powered energy source, compress the shell. The greater the compression, the faster you'll be transported—up to five times the pace of ordinary time for a Jupiter-sized mass, faster for a larger ball of matter.

- After waiting the desired interval—several decades works best—slowly decompress the shell and emerge. You'll find yourself in the same place but in a distant epoch. Welcome to the future.

Fine print: This is a relatively slow method of time travel, and life inside the shell could become tedious.

Van Stokum Cylinder

Mass and energy act on space-time like a rock thrown into a pond: the bigger the rock, the bigger the ripples. Physicist W. J. van Stockum realized in 1937 that an immense cylinder spinning at near-light speed will stir space-time as though it were molasses, pulling it along as the cylinder turns. Although Van Stockum himself didn't recognize it, anyone orbiting such a cylinder in the direction of the spin will be caught in the current and, from the perspective of a distant observer, exceed the speed of light. The result: Time flows backward.

Circle the cylinder in the other direction with just the right trajectory, and this machine can take you into the future as well. How it works:

- Using a high-performance spacecraft with tractor beams, or at least heavy-duty cables, trawl the galaxy gathering planets, asteroids, comets, and the like. Collect as much matter as you can.
- With a galactic-scale forge, extrude the planetary matter into a long, dense cylinder.
- Use an industrial-strength electromagnetic field to spin the cylinder along its central axis. Accelerate it to the speed corresponding to your destination time.
- Orbit the cylinder in the direction of the spin. With each circuit you make, you'll return at a time before you left.

Fine print: The cylinder must be infinitely long, which could add slightly to its cost.

Kerr Ring

When Karl Schwarzschild solved Einstein's equations in 1917, he found that stars can collapse into infinitesimally small points in space—what we now call black holes. Four decades later, physicist Roy Kerr discovered that some stars are saved from total collapse and become rotating rings. Kerr didn't regard these rings as time machines. However, because their intense gravity distorts space-time, and because they permit large objects to enter on one side and exit on the other in one piece, Kerr-type black holes can serve as portals to the past or the future. If finding one with the proper dimensions is too much trouble, you can always build one yourself:

- Gather enough matter to equal Jupiter's mass.

- Compress it into a ring about 5 feet in diameter. This can put a lot of stress on mechanical tools, so a high-energy electromagnetic field is recommended.

- As you compress the ring, set it spinning. Increase its velocity to nearly the speed of light. A black hole will form at its center.

- Step through the hole and you'll be transported instantly to another time (and, possibly, place), potentially as far back as the big bang or as far forward as the end of the universe as we know it. Bon voyage!

Fine print: The Kerr ring is a one-way ticket. The black hole's gravity is so great that, once you step through it, you won't be able to return.

Web Sites

Due to the changing nature of Internet links, the Rosen Publishing Group, Inc., has developed an online list of Web sites related to the subject of this book. This site is updated regularly. Please use this link to access the list.

http://www.rosenlinks.com/cdfp/quph

For Further Reading

Ford, Kenneth W. *The Quantum World: Quantum Physics for Everyone.* Cambridge, MA: Harvard University Press, 2004.

Greene, Brian. *The Elegant Universe: Superstrings, Hidden Dimensions, and the Quest for the Ultimate Theory.* New York, NY: W. W. Norton, 1999.

Halpern, Paul. *The Great Beyond: Higher Dimensions, Parallel Universes and the Extraordinary Search for a Theory of Everything.* Hoboken, NJ: Wiley, 2004.

Hey, Tony, and Patrick Walters. *The New Quantum Universe.* New York, NY: Cambridge University Press, 2003.

Kaku, Michio. *Einstein's Cosmos: How Albert Einstein's Vision Transformed Our Understanding of Space and Time.* New York, NY: W. W. Norton, 2004.

Veltman, Martinus. *Facts and Mysteries in Elementary Particle Physics.* River Edge, NJ: World Scientific, 2003.

Zee, A. *Quantum Field Theory in a Nutshell.* Princeton, NJ: Princeton University Press, 2003.

Bibliography

Bohm, David. *Causality and Chance in Modern Physics.* Philadelphia, PA: University of Pennsylvania Press, 1999.

Brooks, Michael. "The Weirdest Link." *New Scientist,* Vol. 181, No. 2440 (March 27, 2004): pp. 32–35.

Cassidy, David, and the Center for History of Physics. "Quantum Mechanics, 1925–1927." American Institute of Physics Web site, November 1998. Retrieved October 15, 2004 (http://www.aip.org/history/heisenberg/p08.htm).

Clarke, John. "Superconductivity: A Macroscopic Quantum Phenomenon." *Beam Line,* Vol. 30, No. 2 (Summer/Fall 2000): pp. 41–48.

Dowling, Jonathan P., and Gerard J. Milburn. "Quantum Technology: The Second Quantum Revolution." *Philosophical Transactions of the Royal Society of London,* Vol. 361, No. 1809 (2003): 1655–1658.

Gourley, Paul L. "Nanolasers." *Scientific American,* Vol. 278, No. 3 (March 1998): pp. 56–61.

Herdeiro, Carlos. "M-Theory, the Theory Formerly Known as Strings." Cambridge Relativity & Gravitation Research Web site, 1996. Retrieved

October 15, 2004 (http://www.damtp.cam.ac.uk/user/gr/public/qg_ss.html).

Kaku, Michio. "A User's Guide to Time Travel." *Wired*, No. 11.08 (August 2003).

Kaku, Michio. *Visions: How Science Will Revolutionize the 21st Century.* New York, NY: Anchor Books, 1997.

Kaku, Michio, and Jennifer Trainer Thompson. *Beyond Einstein: Superstrings and the Quest for the Final Theory.* New York, NY: Oxford University Press, 1997.

Kleppner, Daniel, and Roman Jackiw. "One Hundred Years of Quantum Physics." *Science*, Vol. 289, No. 5481 (2000): pp. 893–898.

Leggett, Tony. "Quantum Theory: Weird and Wonderful." *Physics World*, Vol. 12 (December 1999): pp. 73–77.

Lightman, Alan P. *Great Ideas in Physics: The Conservation of Energy, the Second Law of Thermodynamics, the Theory of Relativity, and Quantum Mechanics.* New York, NY: McGraw-Hill, 2000.

Siegfried, Tom. *The Bit and the Pendulum: From Quantum Computing to M Theory—The New Physics of Information.* New York, NY: Wiley, 2000.

Smolin, Lee. "Atoms of Space and Time." *Scientific American*, Vol. 290, No. 1 (January 2004): pp. 67–75.

Weiss, Peter. "Quantum Internet: Possible Use of Quantum Mechanics in Computer Networks." *Science News*, Vol. 155, No. 14 (April 3, 1999): pp. 220–221.

Zeilinger, Anton. "Fundamentals of Quantum Information." *Physics World*, Vol. 11 (March 1998): pp. 35–40.

Zeilinger, Anton. "Quantum Teleportation." *Scientific American*, Vol. 282, No. 4 (April 2000): pp. 50–59.

Index

About the Editor

Fannie Huang completed her undergraduate study in chemistry at Rutgers University in 1995, and has since maintained a strong interest in quantum mechanics and quantum ideas as they pertain to biophysical problems. She is currently working on her doctorate in molecular pathology at Columbia University.

Photo Credits

Front cover (clockwise from top right): "Infinite Textures" © Comstock Images, Quantum bubbles © www.ecliptic.ch © Photo Researchers, Inc.; "Liquid Crystal" © Getty Images; background image of gyroscope © Getty Images; portrait, Isaac Newton © Library of Congress, Prints and Photographs Division. Back cover: top image "Electrons Orbiting Nucleus" © Royalty-Free/Corbis; bottom "Liquid Crystal" © Getty Images.

Designer: Geri Fletcher; Series Editor: Brian Belval